Why Study the Media?

Why Study the Media?

Roger Silverstone

SAGE Publications
London · Thousand Oaks · New Delhi

ISBN 0-7619-6453-3 (hbk)
ISBN 0-7619-6454-1 (pbk)

First published 1999

SAGE Publications Ltd
1 Oliver's Yard
55 City Road
London EC1Y 1SP

SAGE Publications Inc
2455 Teller Road
Thousand Oaks
California 91320

SAGE Publications India Pvt Ltd
B–42 Panchsheel Enclave
PO Box 4109
New Delhi 110 017

British Library Cataloguing in Publication data
A catalogue record for this book is available from the British Library

Library of Congress Control Number: 9972870

Printed digitally and bound in Great Britain by
Lightning Source UK Ltd., Milton Keynes, Bedfordshire

For Jennifer, Daniel, Elizabeth and William

Contents

Preface and acknowledgements

Just how to begin. Now that I have completed it. Perhaps by re-reading my initial proposal. To remind myself of what it was that I set out to do. And not to do.

This was to be a book about the media, but not about media studies, at least not about media studies as it is often seen to be. It was to be a book which would argue for the central importance of the media in culture and society as we enter the new millennium. It was to be a book which raised difficult questions and which tried to define different agendas for those of us who are concerned with the media, but it would not seek too many answers. Openness rather than closure was the aim.

We cannot escape the media. They are involved in every aspect of our everyday lives. Central to the project as a whole was a desire to place the media at the core of experience, at the heart of our capacity or incapacity to make sense of the world in which we live. Central, too, was a desire to claim for the study of the media an intellectual agenda that would pass muster in a world too quick to dismiss the seriousness and relevance of our concerns.

I wanted the study of the media to emerge from these pages as a humane as well as a human undertaking. It was to be humane in its concern for the individual and the group. It was to be human in the sense that it would set a distinct logic, sensitive to the historically and sociologically specific and refusing the tyrannies of technological and social determinism. It would attempt to navigate the boundary between the social sciences and the humanities.

Perhaps, above all, the book was conceived as a manifesto. I wanted to define a space. To engage with those outside my own discourse, elsewhere in the academy and in the world beyond. It was time, I thought, to take the media seriously.

The study of the media needs to be critical. It needs to be relevant. It needs to create and sustain a certain distance between itself and its subject. It needs to be seen to be thinking. I hope that what follows will, at least in some degree, meet these exacting requirements.

However, if it succeeds, even partially, in meeting its objectives, then as much as anything it will be because so many individuals, both colleagues and students, have in direct and indirect ways contributed to it. Let me list them in alphabetical order, with gratitude: Caroline Bassett, Alan Cawson, Stan Cohen, Andy Darley, Daniel Dayan, Simon Frith, Anthony Giddens, Leslie Haddon, Julia Hall, Matthew Hills, Kate Lacey, Sonia Livingstone, Robin Mansell, Andy Medhurst, Mandy Merck, Harvey Molotch, Maggie Scammell, Ingrid Schenk, Ellen Seiter, Richard Sennett, Bruce Williams, Janice Winship and Nancy Wood. None, of course, bears any responsibility for what errors and infelicities may still remain.

1 The texture of experience

Jerry Springer's day-time talk show, 22 December 1998. Repeated for the *n*th time on the satellite channel, *UK Living*. He talks to men who work as women. Two rows of transvestite and transsexual men discuss their lives, their relationships and their work. They are baited by the television audience. They are asked questions about having children. A couple exchange rings: 'After all, we've not done it before and it is national television.' Jerry wraps up with a homily on the normality and lack of seriousness of such behaviour, reminding his audience of Milton Berle and *Some Like it Hot*, of performances in a more innocent age in which drag was not seen as some kind of perversion.

A moment of television. Exploiting but also exploitable. A moment easily forgotten, a sub-atomic particle, a pin-prick in media space, but now, if only here on this page, noticed, noted, felt, fixed. A moment of television which was local (all the characters worked in a theme restaurant in Los Angeles), national (it was originally transmitted in the US) and global (it's over here). A moment of television scratching at the surface of suburban sensibility, touching margins, touching base.

A moment of television which will, however, serve perfectly. It represents the ordinary and the continuous. It is, in its uniqueness, entirely typical. It is an element in the constant media mastication of everyday culture, its meanings dependent on whether we indeed do notice, whether it touches us, shocks, repels or engages us, as we flick in and out and across our increasingly insistent and intense media environment. It offers itself to the passing viewer and to the advertisers who claim his or her attention, increasingly desperately perhaps. And it offers itself to me as the starting-point of an attempt to answer the question – why study the media? It does this contrarily, of course, but also quite naturally, because it raises so many questions, questions that cannot be ignored, questions that emerge from the simple recognition that our media are ubiquitous, that they are daily, that they are an essential dimension of contemporary experience. We cannot evade media presence, media representation. We have come to depend on our media, both printed and electronic, for pleasures and information, for comfort and security, for some sense of the continuities of experience, and from time to time also for the intensities of experience. The funeral of Diana, Princess of Wales is a case in point.

I can note the hours spent by the global citizen in front of the television, alongside the radio, flicking through newspapers and, increasingly, surfing the Internet. I can note, too, how those figures vary globally from North to South and within nations, according to material and symbolic resources. I can note quantities: the global sales of software, variations in cinema attendance and video rental, the personal ownership of desktop computers. I can reflect on patterns of change and possibly, if foolhardy enough, hazard projections about future trends of consumption. But in doing all or any of these things I am skating across the surface of media culture, a surface which is often sufficient enough for those who are concerned to sell, but which is clearly insufficient if we are interested in what media do, as well as what we do with media. And it is insufficient if we wish to grasp the intensity and insistence of our lives with our media. For that we have to turn quantity into quality.

I want to argue that it is because the media are central to our everyday lives that we must study them. Study them as social and cultural as well as political and economic dimensions of the modern world. Study them in their ubiquity and complexity. Study them as contributors to our variable capacity to make sense of the world, to make and share its meanings. I want to argue that we should study the media, in Isaiah Berlin's terms, as part of the 'general texture of experience', a phrase which touches the grounded nature of life in the world, those aspects of experience which we take for granted and which must survive if we are to live and to communicate with each other. Sociologists have long been concerned with the nature and quality of such a dimension of social life, in its possibility and in its continuity. Historians too, at least in Berlin's view, cannot escape their dependence upon it, for their work, like all those in the human sciences, in turn depends on their capacity to reflect upon and understand the other.

The media now are part of the general texture of experience. If we were to include language as a medium, this would ever be so, and we might wish to consider the continuities of speech, writing, print and audiovisual representation as indicative of the kind of answers to the question I am seeking; that without attention to the forms and contents, to the possibilities, of communication, both within and against the taken-for-granted in our everyday lives, we will fail to understand those lives. Period.

Berlin's characterization, of course, is principally a methodological one. The why necessarily involves the how. History is to be a humane undertaking, not scientific in its search for laws, generalizations or theoretical closure, but an activity premised on the recognition of difference and specificity and a realization that the affairs of men (how tragically gendered is the liberal imagination!) require a sort of understanding and explanation somewhat removed from Kantian and Cartesian injunctions for pure rationality and reason. My claim for the study of the media will be thus, and I will also return from time to time to its methods.

Berlin also talks of the appropriate kind of explanation being related to moral and aesthetic analysis:

> in so far as it presupposes conceiving of human beings not merely as organisms in space, the regularities of whose behaviour can be described and locked in labour saving formulae, but as active beings, pursuing ends, shaping their own and others' lives, feeling, reflecting, imagining, creating, in constant interaction and intercommunication with other human beings; in short engaged in all the forms of experience that we understand because we share them, and do not view them purely as external observers. (Berlin, 1997: 48)

His reliance on a sense of our shared humanity is touching, and is at odds, perhaps, with contemporary received wisdom, but without it we are lost and without it the study of the media becomes an impossibility. This, too, will inform my analysis and I will return to it.

There are other metaphors in the attempts to grasp the media's role in contemporary culture. We have thought of them as conduits, offering more or less undisturbed routes from message to mind; we can think of them as languages, providing texts and representations for interpretation; or we can approach them as environments, enfolding us in the intensity of a media culture, cloying, containing and challenging in turn. Marshall McLuhan sees media as extensions of man, as prostheses, enhancing both power and reach, but perhaps, and maybe he saw this, both disabling as well as enabling us as we, both media's subjects and objects, become progressively entwined in the prophylactically social.

Indeed we could think of the media as prophylactically social in so far as they have become substitutes for the ordinary uncertainties of everyday interaction, endlessly and insidiously generating the *as-ifs* of everyday life and increasingly creating defences against the intrusions of the unwelcome or the unmanageable. Much of our public concern about media effects is focused on this aspect of what we see and fear in, especially, the new media: that they will come to displace ordinary sociability and that we are breeding, mostly through our male children, and most especially through our male working-class and black children (still the locus of most of our moral panics), a race of screen junkies. Marshall McLuhan (1964) does not go so far despite his ambivalence. On the contrary. Yet his vision of cyborg culture predates Donna Haraway's (1985) by some 20 years.

These metaphors are useful. Indeed without them we are condemned to look at our media as if through a glass darkly. But like all metaphors the light they throw is partial and ephemeral, and we need to go beyond them. My purpose is to do just that. The answer to my question will involve tracing media through the ways in which they participate in contemporary social and cultural life. It will involve an examination of media as process, as a thing doing and a thing done, and as a thing doing and a thing done at all levels, wherever human beings congregate both in real and in virtual space, where they communicate, where they seek to persuade, inform, entertain, educate, where they seek in a multitude of ways, and with varying degrees of success, to connect one to the other.

To understand media as process, and to recognize that the process is fundamentally and eternally social, is to insist on the media as historically specific. Media are changing, have changed, radically. Our century has seen the telephone, film, radio, television become both objects of mass consumption and essential tools for the conduct of everyday life. We are now confronted with the spectre of a further intensification of media culture, through the global growth of the Internet and the promise (some might say the threat) of an interactive world in which nothing and no one cannot be accessed, instantly.

To understand media as process also involves a recognition that the process is fundamentally political or perhaps, more strictly, politically economic. The meanings that are offered and made through the various communications that flood our everyday lives have emerged from institutions increasingly global in their reach and in their sensitivities and insensitivities. Barely oppressed by the historic weight of two centuries of advancing capitalism and increasingly dismissive of the traditional power of nation states, they have established a platform for, it has to be accepted, *mass* communication. This is, despite its increasing diversity and flexibility, still its dominant form. It constrains and intrudes upon local cultures even if it does not overpower them.

Movements among the dominating institutions of global media are tectonic in scale: gradual cultural erosion and then sudden seismic shifts as multinationals emerge like new mountain ranges from the sea, while others sink and, like Atlantis, are only remembered mythically as once perhaps passably and relatively benevolent. The power of these institutions, the power to control the productive and distributive dimensions of contemporary media, and the correlative and progressive weakening of national governments to control the flow of words, images and data within their national borders, is profoundly significant and unarguable. It is a central feature of contemporary media culture.

Much contemporary debate draws on a sense of the speed of these various changes and developments, but mistakes the speed of technological change, or indeed of commodity change, for the speed of social and cultural change. There is a constant tension between the technological, the industrial and the social, a tension that must be addressed if we are to recognize media as indeed a process of mediation. For there are few direct lines of cause and effect in the study of the media. Institutions do not make meanings. They offer them. Institutions do not change evenly. They have different life-cycles and different histories.

But then we are confronted by another question, and then another and another. Who mediates the media? And how? And with what consequences? How might we understand media as both content and form, visibly kaleidoscopic, invisibly ideological? How do we assess the ways in which the struggles over and within the media are played out: struggles over the ownership and control of both institutions and meanings; struggles over access and participation; struggles over representation; struggles which inform and affect our sense of each other, our sense of ourselves?

We study the media because we want answers to these questions, answers that we know cannot be conclusive, and indeed must not be conclusive. Attractive though it may be, and often superficially persuasive, there is no single theory of the media to be had. Indeed, it would be a terrible mistake to try to find one. A political mistake, an intellectual mistake, a moral mistake. Yet at the same time our concern *with* the media is always at the same time a concern *for* the media. We want to apply what we have come to understand, to engage with those who might be in a position to respond, to encourage reflexivity and responsibility. The study of the media must be a relevant as well as a humane science.

My answers, then, to my own question will be premised on a sense of these complexities, complexities that are at once substantive, methodological and, in the broadest sense, moral. I am dealing, after all, with human beings and their communications, with language and speech, with the saying and the said, with recognition and misrecognition and with media as technical and political interventions in the processes of making sense.

Hence the starting-point. Experience. Mine and yours. And its ordinariness.

Research in the media has often preferred the significant, the event, the crisis, as the basis for its enquiry. We have looked at disturbing images of violence or sexual exploitation and tried to measure their effects. We have focused on key media events, like the Gulf War or disasters, both natural and man-made, to explicate the media's role in the management of reality or the exercise of power. We have focused too on the great public ceremonials of our age to explore their role in the creation of national community. There is a point to all of this, since we have known since Freud how much investigation of the pathological, or even the exaggerated, reveals about the normal. Yet continuous attention to the exceptional provokes inevitable misreadings. For the media are, if nothing else, daily. They are a constant presence in our everyday lives, as we switch in and out, on and off, from one media space, one media connection, to another. From radio, to newspaper, to telephone. From television, to hi-fi, to Internet. In public and in private, alone and with others.

It is in the mundane world that the media operate most significantly. They filter and frame everyday realities, through their singular and multiple representations, providing touchstones, references, for the conduct of everyday life, for the production and maintenance of common sense. And it is here, in what passes for common sense, that we have to ground the study of the media. To be able to think that the life we lead is an ongoing accomplishment, requiring our active participation, albeit so often in circumstances over which we have little or no choice, and in which the best we can do is merely to make do. The media have given us the words to speak, and ideas to utter, not as some disembodied force operating against us as we go about our daily business, but as part of a reality in which we participate, in which we share, and which we sustain on a daily basis through our daily talk, our daily interactions.

Common sense, of course neither singular nor undisputed, is where we must begin. Common sense, both the expression of, and the precondition for, experience. Common sense, shared or at least shareable and the often invisible measure of most things. The media depend on common sense. They reproduce it, appeal to it but also exploit and misrepresent it. And, indeed, its lack of singularity provides the stuff of everyday disputes and dismays as we are forced, as much as anything through media and increasingly perhaps only through the media, to see, to confront, the common senses and common cultures of others. The fear of difference. Middle-class horror at the pages of the yellow or tabloid press. The hasty and arguably philistine dismissal of the aesthetic or the intellectual. The prejudices of nations or genders. The values, attitudes, tastes, the cultures of classes, ethnicities and the rest, which are reflections and constitutions of experience, and as such are key sites for the definition of identities, for our capacity to place ourselves in the modern world. And it is through common sense that we are enabled, if we are indeed enabled, to share and distinguish our lives with and from others.

This capacity for reflection, indeed its centrality, is one that has been noted often enough by those seeking to define the determining characteristics of modernity and post-modernity, yet their own reflections tend towards seeing the reflexive turn more or less exclusively in the specialist texts of philosophy or social science. I want to claim it too for common sense, for the everyday and, indeed, from time to time, even, or perhaps especially, for the media. The media are central to this reflective project not just in the socially conscious narratives of soap opera, day-time chat show or radio phone-in, but also in news and current affairs, and in advertising, as through the multiple lenses of written, audio and audiovisual texts, the world about us is displayed and performed: iteratively and interminably.

What other qualities might we ascribe to experience in the contemporary world and media's role in it?

Forgive me if I find myself engaging in spatial metaphors to attempt to begin an answer, for it seems to me that space does provide the most satisfying framework for addressing the issue. Time too, of course, but time, and it is now a commonplace of post-modern theory, is no longer what it was. No longer a series of points, no longer clearly demarcated by distinctions of past and present and future, no longer singular, no longer shared, no longer resistant. We can say all of this, knowing, however, that such a dismissal is not quite right, or at the very least it is premature; knowing that lives are led in time, and that those lives are finite; knowing too that sequence is still central, that time is not reversible (except, of course, on the screen) and that stories can still be told. We know that we lead our lives through the days, weeks and years; lives marked by the iterations of work and play, of the repetitions of the calendar, and of the *longues durées* of barely perceived and perhaps increasingly forgettable history. Yet the media have a lot to answer for, and especially the latest generation of computer-based media, for whereas the broadcast was always time based, even if programme content was not, the computer game is endless, and the Internet immediate. Can time survive, as Lewis Carroll might once have enquired, such a beating?

So space it must be, at least for the time being. And space in multiple dimensions, accepting perhaps that space is itself, as Manuel Castells (1996) suggests, no more than simultaneous time. Let me propose, and it is not an original idea, that we think of ourselves in our daily lives, and in our lives with the media, as nomads, as wanderers, moving from place to place, from one media environment to another, sometimes being in more than one place at once, as we might, for example, think ourselves to be as we watch the television or surf the World Wide Web. What kinds of distinctions can be made here? What sorts of movements become possible?

We move between private and public spaces. Between local and global ones. We move from sacred to secular spaces and from real to fictional to virtual spaces, and back again. We move between the familiar and the strange. We move from the secure to the threatening and from the shared to the solitary. We are at home or away. We cross thresholds and glimpse horizons. We all do all these things constantly and in none of them, not one of them, are we ever without our media, as physical or symbolic objects, as guides or as traces, as experiences or as *aides-mémoires*.

To switch on the television, or open a newspaper in the privacy of one's own front room, is to engage in an act of spatial transcendence: an identifiable physical location – home – confronts and encompasses the globe. But such an action, the reading or the viewing, has other spatial referents. It links us with others, our neighbours both known and unknown, who are simultaneously doing the same thing. The flickering screen, the flapping page, uniting us momentarily, but at least during the twentieth century quite significantly, in a national community. Yet to share a space is not necessarily to own it; to occupy it does not necessarily give us rights. Our experiences of media spaces are particular and often fleeting. We rarely leave a trace, barely a shadow, as we engage with those, the others, whom we see or hear or read about.

Our daily passage involves movement across different media spaces and in and out of media space. Media offer us structures for the day, points of reference, points to stop, points for the glance and the gaze, points for engagement and opportunities for disengagement. The endless flows of media representation are interrupted by our participation in them. Fragmented by attention and inattention. Our entry into media space is at once both a transition from the quotidian to the liminal and an appropriation by the quotidian of the liminal. The media are both of the everyday and at the same time alternatives to it.

What I am saying is somewhat different from what Manuel Castells (1996: 376ff) identifies as the 'space of flows'. For Castells, the space of flows signals the electronic, but also the physical, networks that provide the dynamic lattice of communication along which information, goods and people move endlessly in our emerging information age. The new society is constructed in its movement, in its eternal flux. Space becomes labile, dislocated from, though still in some senses dependent on, the lives that are led in real places. My starting-point, in recognizing this abstraction, nevertheless prefers to ground a sense of the flux of what he calls 'the information age' in the shifts within and across experience, since that is where they take place: as felt, known and as sometimes feared. *We* move too in media spaces, both in reality and in imagination, both materially and symbolically. To study the media is to study these movements in space and time and to study their interrelationships and, maybe too, as a result, to find oneself less than convinced by the prophets of a new age as well as by its uniformity and its benefits.

So, if to study the media is to study them in their contribution to the general texture of experience, then certain further things follow. The first is the need to recognize the reality of experience: that experiences are real, even media experiences. This puts us somewhat at odds with much post-modern thinking which proposes that the world we inhabit is a world seductively and exclusively one of images and simulations. In this view the world is one in which empirical realities are progressively denied, both to us and by us, in common sense and in theory. In this view we live our lives in symbolic and eternally self-referential spaces which offer us nothing other than the generalities of the ersatz and the hyper-real, which offer us only the reproduction and never the original and in so doing deny us our own subjectivity and indeed our capacity to act meaningfully. In such a view we are challenged with our collective failure to distinguish reality from fantasy, and for the, albeit enforced, impoverishment of our imaginative capacities. In this view the media become the measure of all things.

But we know they are not. We know, if only maybe of ourselves, that we can and do distinguish between fantasy and reality, that we can and do preserve some critical distance between ourselves and our media, that our vulnerabilities to media influence or persuasion are uneven and unpredictable, that there are differences between watching, understanding, accepting, believing in and acting on or out, that we test out what we see and hear against what we know or believe, that we ignore or forget much of it anyway, and that our responses to media, both in particular and in general, vary by individual and across social groups, according to gender, age, class, ethnicity, nationality, as well as across time. We know all this. It is common sense. And if those of us who study the media were nevertheless to challenge such common sense, and we do, properly and continually, it cannot be swept aside without falling into the same trap which we have identified for others: the failure to take experience seriously and to test our own theories against that experience, that is, to test them empirically. Our theories too will never escape the self-referential. They too will become, endlessly, reflexively unreflective.

To address the experience of media as well as media's contribution to experience, and to insist that this is both an empirical as well as a theoretical venture, is easier said than done. This is because, first, our question requires us to investigate both the role of the media in shaping experience and, vice versa, the role of experience in shaping the media. And, second, because it requires us to enquire more deeply into what constitutes experience and its shaping.

So let us grant, then, that experience is indeed shaped. Acts and events, words and images, impressions, joys and hurts, even confusions, become meaningful in so far as they can be related to each other within some, both individual and social, framework: a framework which, albeit tautologically, gives them meaning. Experience is a matter both of identity and difference. It is both unique and shareable. It is both physical and psychological. So much is clear and indeed banal and obvious. But how is experience shaped and how does the media play a role in its shaping?

Experience is framed, ordered and interrupted. It is framed by prior agendas and previous experiences. It is ordered according to norms and classifications that have stood the tests of time and the social. It is interrupted by the unexpected, the unprepared, the event, the catastrophe, by its own vulnerability, by its own inevitable and tragic lack of coherence. Experience is acted out and acted upon. In this sense it is physical, based in the body and on its senses. Indeed, it is the commonness of bodily experience cross-culturally that anthropologists in particular have argued is the precondition for our ability to understand one another. 'Imagination springs from the body as well as from the mind', suggests Kirsten Hastrup (1995: 83), despite the fact that this is rarely noticed. The body in life, its incarnation, is the material basis for experience. It gives us location. It is the, non-Cartesian, locus of action, and the locus, too, of those skills and competences without which we become disabled. This has significant implications for how we approach the media, and for how media themselves intrude into bodily experience, for they do intrude, continually, technologically. Martin Heidegger's notion of *techne* captures the sense of technology *as* skill. Our capacity to engage with media is preconditioned by our capacity to manage the machine. But, as I have already pointed out, we can think of media as bodily extensions, as prostheses, and it is not then too great a step to begin to lose sight of the boundaries between the human and the technical, the body and the machine. Think digital. There will be more to say about media and bodies.

And there is more to bodies than physique. Experience is exhausted neither in common sense nor in bodily performance. No more is it contained in simple reflection on its capacity to order and be ordered. For bubbling beneath the surface of experience, disturbing tranquillity and fracturing subjectivity, is the unconscious. No analysis of the media can ignore it, nor the theories that address it. And so to psychoanalysis.

Yes, but psychoanalysis is big trouble.

Psychoanalysis is big trouble in a number of ways. It offers, and perhaps it does this most forcefully, a way of approaching the disturbing and the non-rational. It forces us to confront fantasy, the uncanny, desire, perversion, obsession: those so-called troubles of the everyday which are represented and repressed, both, in media texts of one kind or another, and which disturb the thin tissue of what passes usually for the rational and the normal in modern society. Psychoanalysis is like a language. It is like film. And vice versa. The shift from clinical theory and practice to cultural critique is fraught with obfuscation and the too-easy elision, often, of the particular and the general, as well as the arbitrariness (masked as theory) of interpretation and analysis. Yet, like the unconscious itself, psychoanalysis will not go away. It offers a way to think about feelings: the fears and despairs, joys and confusions that scratch and scar the quotidian.

Psychoanalysis is big trouble too in so far as it disturbs the easy rationality of much contemporary media theory, cognitive in its orientation, behavioural in its intent. It challenges sociological reduction, though it fails, mostly, to acknowledge the social. It is, or certainly should be, an approach to reinforce a sense of the complexities of media and culture without closing them down. If we are to study the media, then we have to confront the role of the unconscious in the constitution as well as the challenging of experience, and, likewise, if we are to answer the question, why study the media, then part of our answer must be because it offers a route, if not a royal route, into the hidden territories of mind and meaning.

Experience, both mediated and media, emerges at the interface of the body and the psyche. It is, of course, expressed in the social and in the discourses, the talk and the stories, of everyday life, in which the social is constantly being reproduced. To cite Hastrup once again: 'Not only is experience always anchored in a collectivity, but true human *agency* is also inconceivable outside the continuing conversation of a community, from where the background distinctions and evaluations necessary for making choices of actions spring' (Hastrup, 1995: 84).

Our stories, our conversations, are present both in the formal narratives of the media, in factual reporting and fictional representation, and in our everyday tales: the gossip, rumours and casual interactions in which we find ways of fixing ourselves in space and time, and above all in fixing ourselves in our relationships to each other, connecting and separating, sharing and denying, individually and collectively, in amity and in enmity, in peace and in war. It has been suggested (Silverstone, 1981) that both the structure and the content of media narratives and the narratives of our everyday discourses are interdependent, that together they allow us to frame and measure experience. The public and the private intertwine, narratively. This has to be the case. In soap opera and talk show, private meanings are aired publicly and public meanings are offered for private consumption. The private lives of public figures become the stuff of daily soap opera; the actors who play soap opera characters become public figures required to construct a private life for public consumption. *Hola! Hello!*

What's going on here? At the heart of the social discourses which encrust around, and embody, experience, and to which our media have become indispensable, is a process and practice of classification: the making of distinctions and judgements. Classification is then not just an intellectual nor even just a practical matter, but it is one that is, in Berlin's terms, both aesthetic and ethical. Our lives are manageable in so far as there exists a modicum of order, sufficient to provide the kind of securities which allow us to get through the day. However, such order as we are capable of achieving is neutral neither in its conditions nor its consequences, in the sense that our order impacts on the order of others, and in the sense that it will depend on the order, or even the disorder, of others. Here too we confront an aesthetics and an ethics, a politics in essence, of everyday life, for which the media provide us, in significant degree, both tools and troubles: the concepts, categories and technologies with which to construct and defend distances; the concepts, categories and technologies to construct and sustain connections. These tools are perhaps most in evidence, and therefore most contentious, when a nation is, or feels itself, to be at war. But let not this momentary visibility blind us to the daily work in which we, again both individually and collectively, and our media, are constantly and intensely engaged, minute by minute, hour by hour.

Therefore, in so far as the media are, as I have argued, central to this process of making distinctions and making judgements; in so far as they do, precisely, mediate the dialectic between the classification that shapes experience and the experience which colours classification, then we must enquire into the consequences of such mediation. We *must* study the media.

2 Mediation

I have begun to suggest that we should be thinking about media as a process, as a process of mediation. To do so requires us to think of mediation as extending beyond the point of contact between media texts and their readers or viewers. It requires us to consider it as involving producers and consumers of media in a more or less continuous activity of engagement and disengagement with meanings which have their source or their focus in those mediated texts, but which extend through, and are measured against, experience in a multitude of different ways.

Mediation involves the movement of meaning from one text to another, from one discourse to another, from one event to another. It involves the constant transformation of meanings, both large scale and small, significant and insignificant, as media texts and texts about media circulate in writing, in speech and audiovisual forms, and as we, individually and collectively, directly and indirectly, contribute to their production.

The circulation of meaning, which is mediation, is more than a two-step flow from transmitted programme via opinion leaders to the persons in the street, as Katz and Lazarsfeld (1955) argued in their seminal study, though it is stepped and it does flow. Mediated meanings circulate in primary and secondary texts, through endless intertextualities, in parody and pastiche, in constant replay, and in the interminable discourses, both on-screen and off-screen, in which we as producers and consumers act and interact, urgently seeking to make sense of the world, the media world, the mediated world, the world of mediation. But also, and at the same time, using media meanings to avoid the world, to distance ourselves from it, from the challenges, perhaps, of responsibility or care, the acknowledgement of difference.

This inclusiveness within, our enforced participation with, our media is doubly problematic. It is difficult to unlock, difficult to find an origin, difficult to construct a singular explanation of, for example, media power. And it is difficult, probably impossible, for us, as analysts, to step out of media culture, our media culture. Indeed, our own texts, as analysts, are part of the process of mediation. In this we are like linguists trying to analyse their own language. From within, but also from without.

'A linguist no more steps out of the mobile fabric of actual language – his own language, the very languages he knows – than does a man out of the reach of his shadow' (Steiner, 1975: 111). And this is also the case, I maintain, for media. Hence the difficulty. It is a difficulty which is epistemological, concerning the ways in which we claim our understandings of mediation. And it is ethical in so far as it requires us to make judgements about the exercise of power in the process of mediation. Studying the media is a risk, on both counts. It involves, inevitably and necessarily, a process of defamiliarization. To challenge the taken for granted. To dig beneath the surface of meaning. To refuse the obvious, the literal, the singular. In our work, often and properly, the simple becomes complex, the obvious opaque. Shining lights on shadows makes them disappear. It's all in the angles.

Mediation is like translation, in George Steiner's view of it. It is never complete, always transformative, and never, perhaps, entirely satisfactory. It is also always contested. It is an act of love. Steiner describes translation in terms of hermeneutic motion, a four-fold process involving trust, aggression, appropriation and restitution. *Trust* because in initiating the process of translation we identify value in the text we are addressing; a value which we want to understand, claim and communicate to others, to communicate to our own. In this initial act of trust we declare our belief that there is meaning to be had in the text that we are approaching and that the meaning will survive our translation. We can, of course, be wrong. *Aggression* because all acts of understanding are 'inherently appropriative and therefore violent' (Steiner, 1975: 297). In translation we enter a text and claim ownership of its meaning (Steiner is unrepentently sexist in his metaphors), but the *violence* that we do to the meanings of others, even in the gentlest attempts to understand, is familiar enough: our own discourses are studded with claims that media representation is biased, ideological and often simply false. *Appropriation* involves bringing meanings home: the more or less successful, more or less complete, embodiment, consumption, domestication (the terms are all Steiner's) of meaning. This is a process, however, which is incomplete and unsatisfactory without the fourth and final move: *restitution*. Restitution signals revaluation: the reciprocity within which the translator gives meaning back, and maybe in the process adds to it. The original may have disappeared in its pristine glory, but what emerges in its place is something new, certainly; something better, possibly; something different, obviously. No translation, as Jorge Luis Borges in *Pierre Menard* argues, can be perfect, even in its perfection. No translation. And no mediation.

Steiner's reference is to translation, notwithstanding both his and its sensitivities, as a diadic process, a move from one text to another, and for him principally a move across time. It involves the transition between past and present texts. It is a move which involves both meaning and value. Translation is both an aesthetic and an ethical activity.

Mediation seems to be both more and less than translation, as Steiner discusses it. More because mediation breaks through the limits of the textual and offers accounts of reality as well as textuality. It is both vertical and horizontal, dependent on the constant shifts of meanings through three- and even four-dimensional space. Mediated meanings move between texts, certainly, and across time. But they also move across space, and across spaces. They move from the public to the private, from the institutional to the individual, from the globalizing to the local and personal, and back again. They are fixed, as it were, in texts, and fluid in conversations. They are visible on billboards and web-sites and buried in minds and memories. But mediation is less than translation, maybe, because mediation is sometimes less than amorous. The mediator is bound necessarily neither to his or her text nor to his or her object by love, though in individual cases he or she might be. Fidelity to the image or the event is nothing like as strong as it is, or once was, to the word.

A translation is acknowledged and honoured as a work of authorship. Mediation involves the work of institutions, groups and technologies. It neither begins nor ends with a singular text. Its claims for closure, the product of the ideologies and narratives of news, for example, are compromised at the point of delivery by the certain knowledge that the next communication, the next bulletin, the next story or comment or interrogation will move things and meanings on and elsewhere. Steiner's view of translation does not extend beyond the text, despite the recognition of his own place in language. On the other hand, mediation is endless, the product of textual unravelling in the words, deeds and experiences of everyday life, as much as by the continuities of broadcasting and narrowcasting.

So mediation is less than translation precisely in so far as it is the product of institutional and technical work with words and images, and the product too of an engagement with the unshaped meanings of events or fantasies. The meanings that do emerge, or that are claimed, both provisionally and finally (both, of course, and at once, in almost every act of communication) emerge without the intensity of specific and precise attention to language or without the necessity to recreate, in some degree, an original text. Mediation in this sense is less determined, more open, more singular, more shared, more vulnerable, perhaps, to abuse.

Nevertheless the discussion remains relevant, and especially so since what is involved is not the distinction between different kinds of translation: literalism, paraphrase and free imitation which Steiner himself finds both sterile and arbitrary. It is relevant because what is involved is the recognition that the significance of translation lies in the *investment*, both ethical and aesthetic, that is made in it and the *claims* that are made for it and through it. Translation is a process in which meanings are produced, meanings that cross boundaries, both spatial and temporal. To enquire into that process is to enquire into the instabilities and flux of meanings and into their transformations, but also into the politics of their fixing. Such an enquiry provides the model for the few things I want now to say about mediation.

Consider the example of a young television researcher working on a documentary series on life in total institutions, a series which will enquire into the ways in which such institutions, in this case a monastery, socialize new members into a new way of life, into a new rule, a new order. An initial idea and the successful persuasion of the executive producer of its viability have led to lunch with the Abbott in a Soho restaurant. Would he consider letting the production team into the monastery to follow a group of novices as they are prepared for membership of the community? Would he grant the medium of television the rights of representation? The Abbott would consider it. A previous programme elsewhere on the network had been seen as less than successful, but this was an interesting idea, and there appeared to be some rapport between the two men sufficient for the suggestion to be made that the researcher visit the monastery to discuss it further.

A few weeks later the researcher finds himself in a room with the entire community of monks. He presents his programme idea and finds himself being cross-examined. Maybe in innocence, more likely in professional pride, he outlines what he hopes to achieve in the programme, arguing that it will be faithful to their way of life, and not seek to distort or sensationalize. He will spend time living in the community. The film will be carefully and rigorously researched. Their own voices will be heard. He can be trusted to deliver the truth (yes, he said this). He is convincing. It is agreed. The researcher joins the monks for two weeks and follows their routine. He talks to them and eats with them and attends their services. He comes to respect them intensely but does not understand their *faith*. He selects two novices and discusses what will be involved with them. The plan is to make the film over a period of a year to monitor the progress of the noviciate.

The researcher returns to London and briefs the director and the producer. Filming begins and, in due time, it ends. Miles and miles of images, words and sounds to be cut together into a coherent text. The researcher, despite having undertaken many of the on-camera interviews, is no longer now much involved in the production process and watches as the world that he has observed, and the world that he has, albeit imperfectly and incompletely, come to understand, is reconstructed frame by frame. Increasingly impotently he watches the institutional production of meaning: the construction of a narrative; the creation of a text which accords with programme expectations, a text that will fit into the slot in the schedule, that will claim an audience and claim a meaning. He sees a new reality emerging on the back of the old, recognizable, just, at least to him, but increasingly removed from what he believes the monks themselves would know and understand.

This is a translation undertaken in good faith. However, as the emergent meanings cross the threshold between the worlds of mediated lives and the living media, and as agendas change, as television, in this case, imposes, innocently but inevitably, its own forms of expression and its own forms of work, a new, mediated, reality rises from the sea, breaking the surface of one set of experiences and offering, claiming, others.

The programme is transmitted and indeed repeated. Some time later the researcher meets one of the community socially. What did he, did they, think? Diffidently, and somewhat painfully, the reply was clear enough. Disappointment. Regret. Another failure. An opportunity missed. It may have been a documentary but it did not document, it did not reflect or represent their lives or their institution, accurately. The researcher was neither entirely surprised nor shocked. But he was undone by the recognition of failure. Was it his? Was it inevitable? Could there have been any other outcome?

Meanwhile, millions of folk will have watched the programme; many will have taken pleasure in it; and many will have incorporated something of its meaning into their own understandings of the world. Steiner's account of translation does not include the reader or the reading. My account of mediation must do so, for without the privileging of those, all of us, who engage continuously and infinitely with media meanings, and without a concern with the effectiveness of that engagement, then we run the risk of misreading. We all participate in the process of mediation. Or not, as the case may be.

This story of television's documentary engagement with a private world is perhaps familiar enough, and it is increasingly understood both by those approached to participate as subjects in mediation, and by viewers and readers who have come to understand some of the limits in the media's claims for authenticity. At its heart, however, as Steiner recognizes, is the issue of trust. And trust at so many different points in the process. The subjects of the film must trust those who present themselves as mediators. The viewers must trust the professional mediators. And the professional mediators must trust in their own skills and capacities to provide an honest text.

And though we might be excused for seeing such trust as so easily betrayed, cynically or not, it is a precondition for mediation, a necessary precondition in all the media's efforts at representation, and especially factual representation. Clearly this issue of trust is not one that frames all forms of mediation, though it is equally a precondition, as Jurgen Habermas (1970) has argued, for any effective communication. One question that will emerge again and again in this book is what is happening to trust at the heart of the process of mediation, and the realisation of just how important it is to find ways of preserving or protecting it.

We are all mediators, and the meanings which we create are themselves nomadic. They are also powerful. Boundaries are crossed, and once programmes are transmitted, web-sites constructed or e-mails posted they will continue to be crossed until the words and images that have been generated or simulated disappear from sight or from memory. Every crossing is also a transformation. And every transformation is itself a claim for meaning, for its relevance and its value.

Our concern with mediation as a process is therefore central to the question of why we should study the media: the need to attend to the movement of meanings across the thresholds of representation and experience. To establish the sites and sources of disturbance. To understand the relationship between public and private meanings, between texts and technologies. And to identify the pressure points. And we need to be concerned not just with factual reporting, with the media as sources of information. The media entertain. And in this, too, meanings are made and transformed: bids for attention, for the fulfilment and frustration of desire; pleasures offered or denied. But resources always for talk, for recognition, identification and incorporation, as we measure, or do not measure, our images and our lives against those we see on the screen.

We need to understand this process of mediation, to understand how meanings emerge, where and with what consequences. We need to be able to identify those moments where the process appears to break down. Where it is distorted by technology or intention. We need to understand its politics: its vulnerability to the exercise of power; its dependence on the work of institutions as well as individuals; and its own power to persuade and to claim attention and response.

3 Technology

We cannot go far in our concern with the media without enquiring into technology. Our interface with the world. Our face-off with reality. Media technologies, for they are technologies, both hardware and software, come in different shapes and sizes, shapes and sizes that are now changing rapidly and in a bewildering way. They are propelling many of us into the nirvana of the so-called 'information age', while leaving others gasping for breath like drunks on a sidewalk, shuffling through the litter of already obsolescent software and discarded operating systems, or just making do, at best, with plain old telephony and analogue terrestrial broadcasting.

To think about technology, to question it in the context of a concern with media, is no simple matter. And not just because of the speed of change, speed which itself is neither predictable nor uncontradictory in its implications. Much is written about media technology's capacity to determine the ways in which we go about our daily business, the ways in which our capacity to act in the world is both enabled and constrained. We are in the midst, we are told, and truthfully too at least for a small proportion of the world's population, of a technological revolution far-reaching in its consequences, a revolution in the generation and dissemination of information. New technologies, new media, increasingly converging through the mechanism of digitalization, are transforming social and cultural time and space. This new world never sleeps: 24-hour news casting, 24-hour financial services. Instant access, globally, to the World Wide Web. Interactive commerce and interactive sociability in virtual economies and virtual communities. A life to be lived on-line. Channel upon channel. Choice upon choice. Jelly-bean television.

Listen to the voices of Silicon Valley or the Media Lab. Listen, for example, to Nicholas Negroponte (1995: 6):

> Early in the next millennium your right and left cufflinks or earrings may communicate with each other by low orbiting satellites and have more computer power than your present PC. Your telephone won't ring indiscriminately; it will receive, sort, and perhaps respond to your incoming calls like a well trained English butler. Mass media will be redefined by systems for

> transmitting and receiving personalised information and entertainment. Schools will change to become more like museums and playgrounds for children to assemble ideas and socialise with other children all over the world. The digital planet will look and feel like the head of a pin.

What will they say to each other, my cuff links? What will I do with all that computing power? If all my information is personalized, how will I ever learn anything new? Who will pay for the new kind of schools and retrain the teachers (or find other jobs for them when they have gone)? How will I manage the pointed pinpricks of global propinquity?

The problem is how to think this through once, that is, one grants that technology does not come upon us without human intervention. Once one acknowledges that it emerges from complex processes of design and development that themselves are embedded in the activities of institutions and individuals constrained and enabled by society and history. New media are constructed on the foundations of the old. They do not emerge fully fledged or perfectly formed. Nor is it ever clear how they will be institutionalized or used, or even less, what consequences they will have on social, economic or political life. The certainties of a techno-logic, the certainties of cumulative development in, for example, speed or miniaturization, do not produce their equivalent in the realms of experience.

Yet technological change does produce consequences. And such consequences can be, and certainly have been, profound: changing, both visibly and invisibly, the world in which we live. Writing and print, telegraphy, radio, telephony and television, the Internet, each have offered new ways of managing information, and new ways of communicating it; new ways of articulating desire and new ways to influence and to please. New ways, indeed, to make and transmit and to fix meaning.

Technology, then, is not singular. But in what senses is it plural?

Marshall McLuhan would have us see *technology as physique*, as extensions of our human capacity, physically and psychologically, to act in the world. Our media, especially, have extended range and reach, granting us infinite power but also changing the environment in which that power is exercised. Technologies do this by themselves, prostheses for mind and body, total in their impact, unsubtle and non-discriminating in their effects. His appeal in the sixties was based on the novelty and comprehensiveness of his approach. A prophet in his time, in his own land. And still he is. His message of the simplicity of the media's displacement of the message as the site of influence is at one with those who see in the current generation of interactive and network technologies the full realization of the world as medium. For such folk 'the Internet is a model for what we are'. Cyborgs. Cybernauts. Let the fantasies rip. And the fantasies, or at least some of them, are realized. Infinite storage.

Infinite accessibility. Smart cards and retinal implants. Users are transformed by their use. And what it is to be human is just as surely transformed as a result. Click.

The theoretically unsubtle has its value. It focuses the mind on the dynamics of structural change. It makes us question. But it misses the nuances of agency and meaning, of the human exercise of power and of our resistance. It misses, too, other sources of change: factors that affect the creation of technologies themselves and factors that mediate our responses to them. Society, economy, politics, culture. Technologies, it must be said, are enabling (and disabling) rather than determining. They emerge, exist and expire in a world not entirely of their own making.

Yet the appeal is understandable. And what McLuhan both articulates and unreflectively reinforces is pretty much a universal in culture, in which *technology* can be seen *as enchantment*. The phrase is nearly Alfred Gell's. He uses it to describe those technologies, technologies *of* enchantment, which human beings have devised to 'exert control over the thoughts and actions of other human beings' (Gell, 1988: 7), by which he means art, music, dance, rhetoric, gifts, and all those intellectual and practical artefacts that have emerged to allow us to express the full gamut of human passions, i.e. media.

But technology *as* enchantment has a wider reference, for it describes the ways in which all societies, including our own, find in technology a source and site both of magic and mystery. Gell makes this point too. For him, technology and magic are inextricably linked. The spell is cast as the seeds are planted. Future success is both claimed and explained thereby. Indeed, by definition. For technology is not to be understood merely as machine. It includes the skills and competencies, the knowledge and the desire, without which it cannot work. And 'magic consists of a symbolic "commentary" on technical strategies' (Gell, 1988: 8). The cultures that we have created around our machines and our media are just such. In common sense and everyday discourses, and even in academic writing, technologies appear magically, are magic, and have magical consequences, both white and black. They are the focus of utopian and dystopian fantasies which, as they are cast, are believed to assume physical, material form (*Wired*, Silicon Valley's house journal is a case in point). The workings of the machine are mysterious and as a result we mistake both their origin and their meaning. Our use of them is surrounded by folklore, the shared wisdom of groups and societies which desire control over things they do not understand.

So, technology *is* magical and media technologies are indeed technologies *of* enchantment. That over-determination gives media technologies considerable, not to say awesome, power in our imagination. Our involvement with them is suffused by the sacred, mediated by anxiety, overwhelmed, from time to time, by joy. Our dependence on them is substantial. Our despair when we are deprived of access to them – the telephone as 'a life-line', the television as an essential 'window on the world' – is complete. Our excitement when confronted by the new, on occasion, knows no bounds: '4 trillion megs? No!'

In this context, as well as in others, we can begin to see *technology as culture*: to see that technologies, in the sense which includes not just the what but also the how and the why of the machine and its uses, are symbolic as well as material, aesthetic as well as functional, objects and practices. And it is in this context, too, that we can begin to enquire into the wider cultural spaces in which technologies operate, and which give them both their meaning and their power.

Walter Benjamin recognized decisive moments in the history of Western culture with the invention of the photograph and the cinema, moments which even in the context of his own ambivalence, he nevertheless misread as disenchantment. Mechanical reproduction (the first time, of course, in print) is the defining feature of media technology, fracturing the closed and intimate, unapproachable, distant, sacredness of the work of art and replacing it by the images and sounds of mass culture. For Benjamin that meant the possibility of a new politics, as the new, mass viewers of cinematic images were confronted by representations of reality actually in tune with their experience. He writes:

> The film is the art form that is in keeping with the increased threat to his life which modern man has to face. Man's need to expose himself to shock effects is his adjustment to the dangers threatening him. The film corresponds to profound changes in the apperceptive apparatus – changes that are experienced on an individual scale by the man in the street in big-city traffic, on a historical scale by every present-day citizen. (Benjamin, 1970: 252, n.19)

In this case, and in others, media technologies are seen to emerge at points of generalized social, rather than individual, need. Raymond Williams (1974) makes a similar argument in relation to radio. And, furthermore, it is possible to recognize in their maturation the ways in which they express and refract a good deal of the dynamics of the wider culture. Max Weber might have called this an elective affinity, only this time between technological and social change rather than between Protestantism and capitalism. And, if we are not too concerned with discrete lines of causation, we might follow him. Indeed, it is possible to see in the mutual granularity of contemporary cultures, ethnicities, interest groups, tastes, styles and that of the emerging narrowcasting economy yet another expression of the same socio-technical interdependence.

Media technologies can be considered as culture in another related, though contrasted, sense: as the product of a cultural industry, and as the object of the more or less motivated, more or less determining, culture inscribed by the embedding of technologies within the structures of late capitalism. This is the well-known position of Benjamin's erstwhile colleagues, Theodor Adorno and Max Horkheimer (1972). And notwithstanding the uncompromising stridency of their arguments, what they say must be recognized, as it seems once again to be, as an intensely powerful critique of the capacity of the might of capital to betray culture while claiming to defend it, and as a sustained analysis of the cultural forces unleashed by media technologies (and they barely saw television) in manufacturing and sustaining the mass, as commodity, and as entirely vulnerable to the blandishments of a totalizing industry that leaves nothing, not even the starlet's curl, out of range. We know this, even if we come to value it differently.

There is no escape here. It is the technology which wins, poisoning originality and value, offering banality and monotony in their place. The critique is of the cinema not of individual films; of recorded music, especially jazz, and not of individual songs. All represent the industrialization of culture: the ersatz, the uniform and the inauthentic. And it is, fundamentally, a critique of technology as culture, and of technology as culture as unthinkable outside the political and economic, especially the economic, structures that contain it, and on whose anvil its daily output is forged.

Yet we can think of *technology as economics* in another way. And not just as an economics of media technology, an economics which in turn depends on a concern with markets and their freedom, with competition, with investment, and with the costs of production and distribution, research and development. Such an economics involves an application of wider economic theory and practice to the specific domain of media and technology, though even here, from the very beginning, changes in technology have forced economists to rethink principles and categories, not least as a result of the production of the world market, and the globalization of information without which such a market could not be sustained. The market in information is quite different from the market in tangible goods. There are no costs in its reproduction, and increasingly fewer costs in its distribution. The economics of public service broadcasting, of universal access, of spectrum scarcity and then in a post-digital age, of its abundance, have emerged as media and information technologies themselves have emerged, and as they in turn continue to challenge and transform received economic wisdom.

This is nowhere more true than in the sphere of Internet economics where, arguably, information is both the commodity as well as the principle of its management. The new economics has to deal with issues such as security, data protection, standards and the enforcement of intellectual property rights. It has to come to terms with an economic space which is defined by a rapidly expanding and still relatively open information environment in which commerce, electronic commerce, takes place; an environment on which it depends. As Robin Mansell (1996: 117) notes: 'Increasingly, businesses are establishing commercial services on the Internet and many of these services support the information elements of electronic commerce.' The loop. Information to information. Money to money. But how to get some of it?

At a workshop at the University of California, European academics meet representatives of Silicon Valley: the entrepreneur, the lawyer, the economist, the financial analyst, the journalist and the chronicler. There are both advocates and critics but the participants are united by their insider status, and they speak, for all the world, in tongues. Yet what emerges from those two and a half days of talk is a vision of a new economy, not of course unrelated to the old one but driven now by new principles and practices, both of which are seen to be emerging from the trial and error of money-making on the Internet. In this world the future is unknown, the past barely remembered and in any event pretty irrelevant. The present is the only concern. Suffused by the evolutionary ideologies of US culture, in which Darwin reigns as much in economic and social space as in the realms of biology, and in which individual actors fight for economic survival in a game whose rules only emerge as a result of their actions and not as their precondition – yet another new frontier – the discussion turns on the ways in which the Internet itself is becoming a consumer product.

The consumer sphinx. Empowered by a supposedly friction-free economy in which choices among products are infinite, information about them is accessible and clear and our capacity to decide between them (at last) rational, our purchase decisions, both as individuals and institutions, are deemed to be unconstrained by anything other than our capacity to pay. Yet this empowerment is, in the same breath, compromised by the various strategies that firms, both the global and the local, are developing to recruit and constrain our choices. Our purchase decisions are logged, preferences ascertained, tastes defined, loyalties claimed. The talk is of compaks (service, buy-back and upgrade agreements that keep us hooked to a particular product), cliks (bundles of information collated about our on-line purchase decisions, matching economic behaviour with the patterns of site access, which allow highly personalized marketing) and zags ('Zip, age and gender, and you've got him (or her)').

The talk is also of 'following the free': giving the initial software out without charge, and making money on upgrades, more sophisticated information or secondary products. Razors and razor blades. Netscape, Bloomberg. Microsoft. It is of the challenges of an over-heating technological space in which product cycles are measured in months rather than years, and of the risk that consumers will begin to realize (maybe they already have) that the last upgrade was, indeed, going to be the last. That the bandwagon of greater power and increasing speed would begin to slow down, and that consumers would begin to tire. Surely not. And it is of the *volkscomputer*, the minimalist solution to the problems of complex technology. Who will be the next master or mistress of the hardware industry, its Henry or Henrietta Ford?

We learn about the markets: that the video games business is now bigger than Hollywood; that the on-line karaoke market in Japan is worth $2bn. We learn about the emergence of spot markets for the purchase of bandwidth on ADSL lines. We discuss anti-trust, copyright and intellectual property. What exactly is a copy in cyberspace? And we discuss the brand, always the brand. The power of the name, the signifier of a global product, the location of the new aura. God, the brand. Brand, the god. Nike, the spirit of victory. The deity in whom we trust. The source of community, and health and potency and success, which *only* exists, *contra* Benjamin, in its massive, insatiable reproduction. From quantity to quality. Intel inside (and Intel is indeed inside, preloaded into my spell-check dictionary. Good old Microsoft.). Follow me. Follow me. Buy me.

And it is not just the multinationals that can play this game. Little folk can have brands too. '*I'm* a brand', says one contributor. 'My book on Silicon Valley has sold 700,000 copies world wide. I have a regular column on the PBS web-site. I sell my services as a consultant. I have a TV series and I am developing a start-up software business.' His business card reads 'writer, broadcaster, computerguy' and shows a computer side-on with a wagging tongue emerging from the screen and arms waving wildly from both sides of the monitor.

The metaphors run thick and fast as the discussion pursues continuities and discontinuities between the present and what little is known or recollected of the past. Proctor and Gamble are still there, only this time on web-sites and not soap operas. And so is Microsoft, the axle around which the Internet is beginning to turn, and the provider of a global software infrastructure upon whose platforms smaller software producers are developing their own proprietary products. It is as if a natural monopoly is beginning to emerge and that, *force majeure*, one global company is building all the roads on which the rest of us must travel. Or maybe not. The future, at least here, will be left to take care of itself; as will the market. For in California, or so it seems, the price of failure is small, the possibilities to restart real, and the prizes of success are beyond measure. That is for the big firms and for the little ones: those with muscle and those with guile; those that can buy ideas and those that actually have them. It is those in between who will find the going hard.

If this is true then we can see the same thing happening elsewhere, in political space as well as in economic space. There is a detectable tendency for the new media to create a society with an excluded middle, in which in both the world of economic as well as political organizations, the mediating centre, the mid-sized firm and indeed the nation state, are being squeezed out of contention by the forces of the large and the small, the global and the local.

Indeed in the world of the Internet, as well as in wider media space, *technology* can also be seen *as politics*. And this in two dimensions. The politics that emerges or can be argued for *around* the media is a politics of access and regulation, and the politics that may or may not be enabled *within* the media is a politics of participation and representation, in both senses of the word, in which new forms of democracy might emerge; or indeed, new forms of tyranny.

Much has been made, over the years, of the effects of television, especially, on the political process; much too of the combined effects of media, commodification and the rising bourgeois state on the possibility for genuine democratic discourse. In both cases the technologies are necessary but not necessarily sufficient conditions for change. They only operate in context. Yet in our new media environment there are hopes that from the unlikely beginnings of the interactive anarchy that is the Internet in its still relatively free state, there will emerge new forms of responsive and participatory politics which are relevant both to the global community and to the local one. On-line democracy, electronic town halls and referendums, these are the stuff of the new political rhetoric which does indeed see technology as politics. Yet such hopes are themselves dependent on a more conventional politics which will, or will not, produce policies for access, defining and guaranteeing some form of universal service, protecting privacy and freedoms of speech, managing the concentration of ownership and in general securing the fruits of electronic space for the general social good.

Media and information technologies are ubiquitous and invisible. Indeed, increasingly, they are both, as micro-processors disappear inside one machine after another, monitoring, regulating, managing how they work, what they will do for us, creating and maintaining their connections to other equally invisible machines. The computer, as such, or indeed the television, may rapidly become a thing of the past. *Technology as information*. Caught in the net.

In our dependence on, and our desire for, technology, we, the users and consumers, collude with this. We understand it. Perhaps we even need it. We do not need to see the machine or understand its workings. Just let it work. Just let it work for us. Culture is, in significant part, a matter of taming the wild. We do this with our machines, with our information, as much as we have done it in the past with our animals and our crops. In this activity there is both logic and magic. Security and insecurity. Confidence and fear.

We need to understand technology, especially our media and information technologies in just such a context if we are to grasp the subtleties, power and consequences of technological change. For technologies are social things, suffused with the symbolic, and vulnerable to the eternal paradoxes and contradictions of social life, both in their creation and in their use. The study of the media, I maintain, in turn requires such a questioning of technology.

Textual claims and analytical strategies

In this section the focus is on the ways in which the media claim us. At its heart, of course, is a concern with media power, with its effectiveness as well as with its effects. The claims are claims for attention, but also for response. Our mediated world is rapidly overflowing with messages and calls to be heard; a surfeit of information, a surfeit of pleasures, a surfeit of persuasions, to buy, to vote, to listen. Billboards, radio, television, magazine and newsprint, the World Wide Web, all jostling for space, time and visibility: to catch a moment, to touch a nerve, to release a thought, a judgement, a smile, a dollar.

The focus is on the mechanics of mediation; the techniques if not the technologies that drive the media into our lives. How to capture the glance? To engage the intellect? To seduce the spirit? The media's texts are texts like any other. The means for analysing them and the questions we ask of them are no different in essence from questions that have been asked about other texts at other times. The fact that they are in some sense popular, that they are in some sense ubiquitous, or ephemeral, does not disqualify this kind of enquiry. On the contrary, we can use the analytical tools that have served us well elsewhere. We need to know *how the media work*: what they offer us and how. And the starting-point for such an enquiry is in the texts themselves and their claims.

One can approach this enquiry in a multitude of ways, through the detail of the hourly and daily shifts of character and content, or through the consistencies and insistencies of structure and form. I am interested in the latter. In media analysis the devil is not in the detail. Soap operas and news bulletins come and go, and enchanted though we may be with the minutiae of character or situation it is the production of that enchantment which needs to be explained. Even the exceptional, the event or the catastrophe, the unique and transcendent moments of contemporary culture, are framed and displayed through familiar forms, arguably containing the disturbance that they may cause, domesticating them as well as exploiting or sensationalizing them.

In this section I focus, then, on the three principal mechanisms of textual engagement: rhetoric, poetics and the erotic. Each in turn enables attention to a particular quality of media as they seek to persuade, please and seduce us. Rhetoric, poetics and the erotic are both textual and analytical strategies. All texts employ such strategies in one way or another, and in different degrees. However, if we are to make sense of the complexities of textual appeal and media power, we have to think analytically, for texts engage us in different ways and with different calls on our sensibilities. Emotions are as important as intellect. The superficial as much as the profound. And there are different kinds of engagement. We consume our media in different ways, often without reflection: stupefied as well as alert; active, often, only in terms of our desire and capacity to surf across media spaces, flicking the remote or clicking the mouse. What spaces do our media offer us and what do we do within them? How do they work and what work do we do in response?

4 Rhetoric

Rhetoric is both practice and critique. To speak well and to some purpose, and to understand and teach how best to do it. Rhetoric, memory and invention. Inextricably intertwined, they once formed the basis of an oral, public culture: enabling expression, enhancing creativity, ennobling thought: to instruct, to move, to please. Rhetoric appeared to die with the Enlightenment; it became ornamental. We now talk of mere rhetoric, suspicious of the artifice of the well-turned phrase or the stunning metaphor. But we also bewail its loss in the speech-making of politicians and other public figures, imprisoned, as they increasingly seem to be, by the sound-bite and the filibuster.

Above all, rhetoric is persuasion. It is language oriented to action, to the change of its direction and to its influence. It is also language oriented to the change of attitude and value. To move but also to bend: 'Rhetoric is rooted in the essential function of language itself, a function that is wholly realistic and is continually born anew, the use of language as a symbolic means of inducing cooperation in beings that by nature respond to symbols' (Burke, 1955: 43).

I want in this chapter to explore rhetoric as a dimension of media, which palpably it is, and as a means for the analysis of media, which arguably it must become. I want to suggest that the spaces which the media construct for us in public and in private, in our ears, our eyes and our imagination, are constructed rhetorically, and that if we are to make sense of how the media make their claims upon us we can do worse than turn, albeit not slavishly, to the principles at least that underpinned both the performance and the analysis of the first expressions of public oral culture. I want to suggest that the language of media is rhetorical language, and that the presumption of the desire to influence, as well as the acceptance of a hierarchy in the structure of media communication, is a more appropriate presumption than that, for example, which underpins Jurgen Habermas's (1970) view that language is or should be only a language of equality and mutuality.

Indeed, as many writers acknowledge, persuasion implies freedom. It makes no sense to try to persuade someone who cannot choose, who cannot exercise at least a modicum of free will. Persuasion also implies difference since, equally, there is no point in trying to influence someone who already thinks like you do, except perhaps as a kind of ideological top-up. Rhetoric is built on hierarchy, on an acknowledgement of such difference. It involves classification and argument, and not just persuasion. It is speech, but also writing. It was crucial, once, to the composition of 'letters and petitions, sermons and prayers, legal documents and briefs, poetry and prose, but [also] to the canons of interpreting laws and scripture, to the dialectical devices of discovery and proof' (McKeon, 1987: 166). And, it could be argued, it still is.

There is, therefore, no contradiction between rhetoric and democracy, or between rhetoric and knowledge. On the contrary, rhetoric both presumes democracy and requires it; and in so far as rhetoric is both practice *and* critique, then it also sustains it. Rhetoric is central both to the exercise of power and to its opposition. Likewise, in so far as rhetoric is at the heart of both classification and communication, defined and performed as it is through its five branches – invention, arrangement, expression, memory and delivery – then it also presumes that, in whatever contemporary guise, there *is* something to be communicated.

I shall not therefore be discussing mere rhetoric.

Zeno of Citium, in distinguishing rhetoric from logic, describes rhetoric as an open fist, quite different from the closed fist of logic. 'Eloquence', Cicero reports him as saying, 'was like the open palm.' Michael Billig (1987: 95), who cites this, finds in the metaphor an important methodological truth, that argument can be other than the tight fist of logic, that rhetoric marks a space of dispute and debate, a form of argument that does not suffer the sometimes arbitrary closure of a rigorous logic. The open fist signals recognition that in the world of human beings, in matters, for example, of law, politics or ethics, there will always be differences of opinion, with no guarantee of their resolution.

There is, however, another way of exploring Zeno's metaphor which has direct relevance both to the media and to my own argument. It is to see in the open fist a claim, a request, a call for attention. It is to recognize that rhetoric does not guarantee success, that the orator can assume but not insist on an audience, that the argument or the appeal can be ignored. The open fist does not determine. It invites. Rhetoric requires an audience but it cannot invent one. The oration, the text, has, at least, to be not just listened to, but heard.

We live in a public culture in which audiences are at a premium, where attention is at a premium, and where our media offer, endlessly and insistently, an open fist: engaging, claiming, beseeching attention, commercially, politically, aesthetically. Our concern must be with the mechanisms by which this is done: with the ways in which advertisers go about their business, as well as the way in which party politics is conducted; but also with the way that factual media claim their truths and their realities. We must be concerned with the relationship between textual strategies and audience responses, with the *rhetoricization* of public culture, and we must be in a position to do so both analytically and critically.

When Habermas (1989) bewailed the refeudalization of the public sphere, the destruction of the fragile and ephemeral (and arguably imaginary) space which the male members of the bourgeoisie in late eighteenth-century Britain created in the press and in their coffee houses for discussion and debate, a destruction consequent upon the combined forces of media, commodification and the intrusive state, he both recognized and misread the re-emergence of media rhetoric as a dominant force in public life. John Reith, perhaps, understood it better when he formulated the BBC's mission as to inform, educate and entertain. So too did Guy Debord (1977), when he railed against the society of the spectacle.

Consider, however, perhaps the most fundamental rhetorical achievement of our contemporary media, indeed of all media, and especially the factual media: its capacity to persuade us that what it represents actually took place. Both news and documentary make equivalent truth claims. They can be expressed, as Michael Renov (1993: 30) indicates, as 'Believe me, I'm of the world.' Documentary consists in its ability to mobilize ethical, emotional and demonstrative proofs: the worthiness of an argument, the tug of the heart strings, the coherence of the bar chart. In what sense, as Jean Baudrillard (1995) asks, did the Gulf War *not* take place?

And not just the Gulf War. One can reflect on that fateful night in 1968 when Neil Armstrong and Buzz Aldrin set foot on the moon. In a studio in Wembley, North London, a group of young researchers and producers, who had been busy for days, were putting the final touches to a live programme that would bring the first pictures of the moon landing, equally live, to the nation's viewers. The programme which preceded the expected images involved the creation of a studio discussion with invited experts, of course, and what was probably the first television phone-in in the UK: a process, it might be suggested, in which the wild beyond was being claimed, and tamed, for domestic consumption. Hours of waiting and discussion, endless anxieties behind the scenes, preceded the eventual transmission of the pictures, live by satellite; pictures that were both entirely strange but also strangely familiar. Pictures but also words: hazy but readable and hearable; shadow puppets and frail but ominous voices. The claims of history. Its sights and its sounds. The voices-over telling us what was going on; insisting on its significance, interpreting the fuzz, and returning us, from time to time, to mission control.

The production team, once freed from the labours of personnel management and the flood of telephone calls, assembled in a side studio to watch. They had the benefit of a huge Eidofor screen which magnified the granularity of the image but at the same time enveloped the studio space. There was a sense in which they were actually participating, that in some mysterious way they had contributed to the event: that *they* were putting the men on the moon.

Later that night, as others took responsibility for the continued reporting, the researchers left. As one of them walked home he could see the flickering blue lights of televisions still on in the front rooms of flats and houses along the street. He reflected then, as he does now, on the nature of that, mediated, experience, and on the capacity of television, but also radio both then and before, to claim its reality and to ascribe significance to it. How did we know that what we were watching was actually taking place, and not being played out on a vacant lot somewhere in Hollywood or Florida? How did we judge its importance?

Partly, of course, the answer lies in our trust in the institutions responsible for bringing us the story, the trust in abstract and technical systems that is a crucial component of modernity. But partly also the answer lies in the conventions of representation, in the forms of expression, in the fragile but effective balance between the familiar and the new, the expected and the unexpected, the security and reassurance of the narrative and the voice; it lies in the language, the rhetoric, of the emergent text and in its support by other texts before and after, those that continually re-emphasize and reassert the claimed reality. The rhetoric in this case occupied the space, and offered a link, between event and experience, as it always will attempt to do. We were led to believe in something of which we have no independent evidence. Then and now, and forever, it is the text that calls and claims us. 'Believe me. I'm of the world.' And the untrustworthy image is silenced by the embedded rhetoric of an insistent voice.

But clearly this was not just about believing in something taking place beyond reach, but also about being persuaded of its significance and its meaning. The moon landing was the dawn of a new age; the triumph, as the Cold War still ran its course, of good over evil and of the superiority of Western technologies and human bravery over those of the East. In this, too, we were being asked to believe. And, for a moment, perhaps, most of us did.

Rhetoricians, both the old and the new, have noted that rhetoric, if it is to be effective, has to be based on some degree of identification between the orator and the audience. You persuade someone only in so far as you talk their language. To change an opinion requires the yielding to others. At the heart of persuasion, and at the root of rhetoric, are the commonplaces, the *topoi*, without which there can be no connection, without which there can be no creation: neither memory nor invention. The commonplaces are those ideas and values, frames of meaning, which are shared and shareable by speakers and listeners. They are the familiar on which the novel is based, the obvious and the taken for granted on which surprises are built and attention claimed. They draw on the shared understandings and memories of the participants, but they enable those memories to be challenged and reformed. The commonplaces are where rhetoric meets and exploits common sense, sometimes through cliché, often through stereotype, mustering a framework of cognition and recognition without which attempts at persuasion are fruitless. Where do commonplaces come from? This is Richard McKeon (1987: 34): 'Whereas the rhetoric of the Romans took its commonplaces from the practical arts and jurisprudence and the rhetoric of the Humanities took its commonplaces from the fine arts and literature, our rhetoric finds its commonplaces in the technology of commercial advertising and of calculating machines.' The commonplaces are the shared symbols of a community. Shared, though not necessarily undisputed. So disputed but recognizable. Each society will have its own commonplaces, its own reality manifested in the phrases and images of everyday life, plastered on billboards, flickering on screens, together providing frameworks for understanding and prejudice, touchstones for experience and sites for the media rhetorics of the late twentieth century. The commonplaces articulate what might pass for public opinion. They also depend on it.

Rhetoric is technique. One might say it is a technology. Richard McKeon, citing Aristotle in the *Nichomachean Ethics*, calls it 'architectonic': 'an architectonic art is an art of doing. Architectonic arts treat ends which order the ends of subordinate arts' (1987: 3). Its mechanisms are the tropes as well as the figures: the tropes, principally those of metaphor, metonymy, synecdoche and irony; the figures, separated from the trope by no unambiguous divide, which the classical rhetoricians in their different ways enumerated and classified:

> The figures of discourse are the features, the forms or the turns of phrase that are more or less remarkable and more or less privileged in their effect, and through which, in the expression of ideas, thoughts and feelings, discourse deviates more or less from what would have been the simple and common expression. (Todorov, 1977: 99)

As rhetoric declined, it was its figurative rather than its persuasive dimension that came to be the focus of preoccupation. Rhetoric, as Tzvetan Todorov notes, became, imperceptibly, aesthetics: style became ornament; and rhetoric became mere rhetoric.

Yet the figures, 'the lights of thought and language', remain the stuff of eloquence and argument. Cicero lists some, and it might be appropriate to dwell for a moment on his list, if only to invite reflection both on the continuities of expression and the coincidences of mediation that are suggested by it. The point, of course, is not to insist that such classification and analysis is sufficient for an understanding of how our media *work*, but to indicate that whatever literacy we come to define as appropriate to our electronic, secondary, oral culture, that part of it will owe something to classical forms of expression, forms that are part of, but also exceed, the text. So when Stuart Hall and his colleagues (1978) trace the ways in which individual acts of personal violence become 'mugging', and as such a matter of national significance, or Stanley Cohen (1972) writes of the moral panic occasioned by intermittent clashes between mods and rockers in seaside towns, they are engaged, *inter alia*, in rhetorical analysis. We can see the rhetoric at work both within and across the media; above all in that aspect of the rhetorical that we know as amplification. And we can begin to recognize its political significance.

But to Cicero. In Book III of *De Oratore* he discusses style, metaphor, syntax, rhythm, the subconscious effect of style on the audience (and its lapses), and lines of argument:

> For a great impression is made by dwelling on a single point, and also by clear explanation and almost visual presentation of events as if practically going on – which are very effective both in stating a case and in explaining and amplifying the statement, with the object of making the fact we amplify appear to the audience as important as eloquence is able to make it; and explanation is often countered by a rapid review, and by a suggestion that causes more to be understood than one actually says, and by conciseness achieved with due regard to clearness, and disparagement, and coupled with it raillery. . . . (Cicero, 1942: 161–3)

He talks of digression, repetition, reduction, overstatement, understatement, irony, the rhetorical question, hesitation, distinction, correction, preparing the audience for what one is going to do, taking the audience into partnership, impersonation, and so on. He lists figures of speech (*repititio, adiunctio, progressio, revocatio, gradatio, conversio, contrarium, dissolutum, declinatio, reprehensio, exclamatio, immunatio, imago*): all examples of 'actual diction . . . this is like a weapon either employed for use, to threaten and to attack, or simply brandished for show' (Cicero, 1942: 165–7).

One can see here how easy it became, and Todorov points to Cicero himself as the turning point, for the orator to become the rhetorician, and for the rhetorician to become the obsessive classifier of the twists and turns of expression, the train-spotter of verbal styles and fancies. No wonder rhetoric became a dirty word.

It became a dirty word, though in disguise, after its brief revival in the study of media in the 1970s. It was the time of the structuralists and the semioticians digging deeply into the languages of the media, first in film and then in television, exploring structures and forms, examining the conditions for the possibility of meaning (structuralism) and its determination (semiotics). There was virtue in this enterprise, the first sustained attempt to enquire into media power in ways that did not depend on the analysis of effects, but it came a cropper precisely in its presumption of that power. It offered an analysis of meaning at one point of the process, but did not enquire into its consequences nor into the meanings that were enabled as plural, diverse, unstable, contested. It did not feel obliged to investigate the social or the human, to enquire into the indeterminacies at the heart of communication. On the contrary, this was a time, and also later and still, when the human subject, once deemed the source of invention and the proper site of an enquiry into the relationship between media and experience, was disappearing into the structures, both literary and institutional, within which such power was seen as being exercised.

Roland Barthes's classic analysis of the Panzani advertisement in his 'Rhetoric of the Image', one of the earliest sustained analyses of the rhetorics of consumer culture (McLuhan, the arch rhetorician, though, anticipated this attempt by some ten years in his book, *The Mechanical Bride*), offers an account of images as ideology, of the subtle, and not so subtle, ways in which meaning can be conveyed. Rhetoric, indeed, appears 'as the signifying aspect of ideology' (Barthes, 1977: 49). Images were always thought to be untrustworthy. Words were the security. But in the world of mass consumption, neither were seen to be much more than disguises: tricks for the unwary, locations for the locking of the bewitched consumer into texts and product cycles, as well as into the politically incorrect.

I want to suggest, and this will become something of a refrain, that such attention to the media text, to its mechanics and, at this moment, to its rhetorics, is a necessary but insufficient approach for the understanding of mediation in contemporary culture and society. Media literacy (and I will have more to say on this subject in the next chapter) requires no more and no less than other forms of literacy: a capacity to decipher, appreciate, criticize and compose. Is also requires, at least in my perception of it, an understanding of the proper location of the textual claim, historically, sociologically, anthropologically. It requires an appreciation both of mystery and mystification.

'In mystery there must be strangeness; but the estranged must also be thought of as in some way capable of communication' (Burke, 1955: 115). Our eloquent media. What unites Kenneth Burke and Roland Barthes in their analysis of rhetoric is the centrality of class; it is communication across class, across material division, that creates the space for rhetoric: a form of speech, in Burke's eyes, in which the inevitability of hierarchy is masked but also legitimated. Rhetoric creates mystery. Capital exploits it. Persuasion is courtship. The flattery of class and sexual difference. Here is rhetoric as a social product, requiring social analysis as well as textual. Here too is a clue to the rhetorics of popular culture, the perfect flattery.

The roots of rhetoric lie in these fundamental differences of kind, on the one hand, and the desire to communicate across them, on the other. To reach, but also to identify with, an audience. To mobilize the shared commonplaces of the culture of the moment, but to move beyond them, creatively: for commonplaces are the places of invention and innovation as well as memory and memorial.

To examine the texts of the media rhetorically is to examine how meanings are made and arranged, plausibly, pleasingly and persuasively. It is to explore the relationship between the familiar and the new; to decipher textual strategy. But it is also to investigate the audience; to find where and how it is placed in the text; to understand how the commonplaces relate to common sense; how novelty is constructed on familiar bases; and how tricks are turned and clichés mobilized in shifts of taste and style. Advertising is central (and, indeed, a recent exhibition on poster art at the Victoria and Albert Museum in London used the image of the open fist in its own publicity). But so too, as I have suggested, are news and documentary. Public rhetorics in word and image, structured through camera angle and tone of voice, through the familiar forms of representation and reflexivity; the twists of argument, debate, appeal; the articulation of a public culture, never innocent, flattering to deceive; mysterious, mystifying; offering, claiming, challenging, a reality.

My point is that the location of rhetoric has shifted. It has moved from the specificity of the text to the generalities of culture, ubiquitously and insistently visible, ubiquitously and insistently audible. Political campaigns are won and lost, rhetorically, as images and arguments are constructed and managed in one media campaign after another. The surviving Ciceronian military metaphor is telling. Advertising is the industrialization of rhetoric, branding its commodification. News and documentary provide us with the stuff of the real world within forms and structures and tones of voice that persuade us of their veracity and honesty. We have no difficulty, for the most part, in accepting what is said, in accepting, at least, their agenda.

These public rhetorics, strategic in their occupation of the dominant sites of late and global capitalism, must connect with the everyday; the public metaphor with the private. No audience, no connection. No commonplace, no community. But even then no guarantees.

5 Poetics

Stories. We tell them to each other. We have always told them to each other. Stories to comfort, to surprise, to entertain. And there have always been storytellers, sitting by the hearth, travelling from town to town, speaking, writing, performing. Our stories, myths and folktales have defined, preserved and renewed cultures. Narratives of loss and redemption, of heroism and failure. Stories that both manifestly and secretly offer models and morals, routes to the past and the future, guides for the perplexed. Stories that challenge, tease and undermine. Stories with beginnings, middles and ends: familiar structures, recognizable themes, pleasing through their variation; a song well sung, a tale well told, suspense well made. Our stories are both public and private. They appear within the sacred and the profane, claiming reality, playing fantasy, appealing to imagination.

Stories need audiences. Stories need to be heard and read, as well as spoken and written. There is also a claim for community within the telling, a wish for participation, a drawing in, a suspension of disbelief, an invitation to move into and to share, however briefly, another world. And stories live beyond the telling, in dreams and in talk, whispered, retold, time and time again. They are an essential part of social reality, a key to our humanity, a link to, and an expression of, experience. We cannot understand another culture if we do not understand its stories. We cannot understand our own culture if we do not know how, why and to whom our own storytellers tell their tales.

Yet Walter Benjamin, in considering the story in modernity, mourns its decline and finds the source of that decline in the surfeit of information which the media, principally for him the press, do indeed press upon us, isolating us from, rather than connecting us to, experience:

> The replacement of the older narration by information, of information by sensation, reflects the increasing atrophy of experience. In turn, there is a contrast between all these forms and the story, which is one of the oldest forms of communication. It is not the object of the story to convey a happening *per se*, which is the purpose of information; rather, it embeds it in the life of the storyteller in order to pass it on as experience to those listening.

It thus bears the marks of the storyteller much as the earthen vessel bears the marks of the potter's hand. (Benjamin, 1970: 161)

I believe Benjamin to be wrong. We are confronted in contemporary media culture not by the absence of stories but by their proliferation, both within the media's texts and surrounding them. We are increasingly confronted too by the blurring of the boundaries between information and entertainment, facts and stories, a blurring that some find troubling but none of us can ignore. We still have the capacity to relate the products of the media to experience, notwithstanding their capacity for alienation. We still preserve in our culture a profound sense of enchantment. The media enchant. We are, significantly, enchanted. In the western and in the soap opera; in the reporting of the great media events of the day and in the telling of teenage sitcom tales; in our preoccupation with the stars and in our fascination with our origins and futures, the story survives. Indeed, it prospers, drawing, as it now can in our electronic age, on both oral and printed sources; drawing its resources, as it increasingly does, from global cultures; now making serious demands on time and attention, now providing the froth of popular culture: attracting, engaging, cloying, consuming; a commodity in a commercial world.

Stories offer pleasure and they offer order. They require a certain literacy to be heard with pleasure or dismay, as well as a certain literacy for their critique and for an understanding of how they work. And it is this latter kind of literacy, based on the need to understand precisely that connection between media and experience, to understand the relationship between intention and appeal, interest and response, text and action, to understand the mechanisms of media's engagement in our everyday lives, which I am arguing for here. Our stories are social texts: drafts, sketches, fragments, frameworks; visible and audible evidence of our essentially reflexive culture, turning the events and ideas of both experience and imagination into daily tales, on big screens and on small. And in this guise they are our culture, whether we like it or not, expressing the consistencies and contradictions of fantasy and classification, and offering texts for us, their audiences, to position ourselves, to identify with character and tone, to follow the plot, and to take away (or not) something of the narrative's capacity for imitation.

Storytelling is permanently in the subjunctive. It creates and occupies the territory of the 'as-if': inviting wishes, possibility, desire; raising questions, seeking answers. Victor Turner (1969) sees this as a function of ritual, those activities that occupy a liminal space, marked more or less clearly by a threshold separating it from the quotidian. Ritual is both part of, and other than, the everyday. It allows room for play. Stories occupy a similar cultural space.

So when we enquire, as students of the media, into the narrative pleasures offered by a soap opera or a situation comedy we are enquiring into their capacity to articulate something of our common culture. We are seeking to understand the rhythms of their narrative, their characterization, their ways of representing a recognizable world; offering characters – the strong woman, the love-lorn teenager, the sufferer from AIDS, the battered child – and offering situations – divorce, conflicts over money, death – to which audiences can and do relate. And such representing and relating is not always easy to understand, certainly not for those for whom the object of engagement is seen to be beyond the pale, to be without quality. Yet we must try.

But how? Fashions change; in academic enquiry no less than elsewhere. And fashions have changed in the study of media narratives quite significantly over the past 20 years, as the various forms of literary deconstruction have eroded their presumed authority. These have resulted in versions of the world, indeed an aesthetics, which see meanings as having been dispersed, as dispersed as the cultures and identities of those who make them, above all in their reception: as readers, viewers, consumers.

Of course, we have to recognize that the world's discourses, both the popular and the elite, are multiple. They overlap. They converge and diverge. They are unstable. We talk of meanings' traces, the silver threads that snails leave on garden walls. We find meanings being made dialogically, at the interface between text and reader, or conversationally, in the interactivity of Internet talk. We talk of the fracturing of identities in a post-modern age, the indeterminacies of ethnicities, classes, genders and sexualities around which cultures form, offering us one thing now, another later; here, there, everywhere, as we wander through time and space, nomadically. We are seen to be dancers at an endless carnival; masqueraders in and among the hyper-real.

I cannot deny all of this, but I want to suggest that much of it is fancy: an ironic and unreflective projection which ignores, principally, the materiality of both symbol and society. It misreads the capacity of texts to convince, to frame meaning, to give pleasures, to create communities, and it misreads the realities of meaning making and the pleasures claimed and sustained, differently of course across class and age and gender and ethnicity, but nevertheless real for all that.

So I want to argue that texts matter, that stories live, and that media require their own poetics: 'In contradistinction to the interpretation of particular works, [poetics] does not seek to name meaning, but aims at a knowledge of the general laws that preside over the birth of each work'

(Todorov, 1981: 6). A media poetics would enquire into the structures of media discourse, into the principles of its organization and the processes of its emergence. But it would also enquire into how such discourses engage with readers and audiences, how they create the meanings, the pleasures and the structures of feeling which emerge in the conscious and unconscious minds of those who allow themselves even a modicum of enchantment, beside the radio, at the keyboard, in front of the screen.

We could do worse than start with Aristotle.

His enquiry is into the principles that underlie and enable poetry: the tragic, the comic and the epic; and principally the first of these, tragedy. His starting-point is imitation: mimesis. Imitation is, he suggests, natural to humankind. It is what distinguishes us from brute beasts, and it is natural for all human beings to delight in works of imitation. Tragedy, involving as it does, the imitation of serious subjects in a lofty kind of verse, as well as exhibiting men as better than the present day (comedy represents them as worse), is the highest form of imitation. Tragedy contains six parts: spectacle, melody, diction, character, thought and plot, of which plot is the most important:

> Tragedy is an imitation not of persons but of action and life, of happiness and misery. Now happiness and misery take the form of action; the end at which the dramatist aims is a certain kind of activity, not a quality. We have certain qualities in accordance with character, but it is in our actions that we are happy or the reverse. Actors therefore do not perform with a view to portraying character; no, they include character for the sake of the action. (Aristotle, 1963: 13)

Plots are the very soul of tragedy. Plots have a unity, a beginning, a middle and an end, necessarily interrelated. The poet does not describe what has happened, but what might happen, and in this he differs from a historian. And poetry as a consequence is, Aristotle believes, of greater significance than history. Tragedy imitates not only complete actions but also incidents that arouse pity and fear. It makes its strongest impact through the presentation of the unexpected and the marvellous. Complexity is all: peripety and discovery its elements. Its aim is what we might call the suspension of disbelief: 'The plot . . . should be constructed in such a way that, even without seeing the things take place, he who simply *hears the account* of them shall be filled with horror and pity at the incidents' (Aristotle, 1963: 23).

The world, of course, has changed since Aristotle; but not entirely. Mimesis, realism, verisimilitude are at the heart of our poetry too, even if that poetry comes in the form of the situation comedy and the feature film, even if our tragedies and comedies are stripped across the evening schedules and across channels, even if they only appear in press serializations, pulp fiction or rented videos. All of these, with varying degrees of success, and certainly subject to differences of value, require analysis. We need to know how they work.

And we need to do this without falling into the trap of the formalisms that defined poetics as an enterprise in literary theory. While it is perfectly acceptable to see in contemporary narratives echoes of earlier forms, the myths and folktales of pre-literate cultures, while it is impossible to ignore the consistencies of storytelling across cultures and across time, while one can argue that such kinds of stories fulfil similar functions as those of an oral culture, reflecting, refracting, resolving (or at least appearing to resolve) the major and minor dilemmas of life and belief in their host cultures, it would be a mistake to insist that such perspectives exhausted the complexities of our own media culture. For our stories are part of a wider refractory culture, and their passages across cultures, from Hollywood to Teheran, as much as from Broadcasting House to Birkenhead, are far from neutral in their consequences or for their meanings.

The poetics of the media must extend beyond the text and examine the discourses that the texts may stimulate but do not themselves determine. There is a path to be taken between the heavy hand of textual determinism and the equally implausible claims for the capacity of readers to make only their own sense. Such a poetics needs to enquire into the relationship between stories told and their retelling, their amplifications and distortions, in the tales we tell each other in our daily lives. It needs to enquire into the secondary and tertiary and quaternary stories that form like barnacles around the hulls of soap operas or blockbuster features: the stories the tabloid press tells about their characters and the actors and actresses who play them; or the appropriation of such stories, both by the media and in our own talk, into other worlds: into the worlds of politics and sport and the family next door.

Such appropriation in turn depends on the accessibility of the texts that are appropriated, on their transparency, on their naturalness. Jonathan Culler (1975) distinguishes five ways in which such *vraisemblance* is produced in a text, a story or a poem; five ways in which it can be seen to be claiming a certain kind of familiarity, adjusting to readers' expectations, offering a shared world, a shared culture. The first is the claim to be representing the real world, the natural attitude. It is based on the expectation that what is being represented is simple, coherent and true. The second is based on the representation of, and the dependence upon, shared cultural knowledge, a knowledge that might be specific to one society rather than another, and subject to change, but which nevertheless is seen as natural in an obvious and self-evident way by those who are its members. Such textual appeals are culturally specific and depend, for example, on the presence of cultural stereotypes. We might see this aspect of *vraisemblance* as ideological.

The third is dependent on genre, or textual conventions which mark one narrative or another as being of a particular kind, and as such recognizable to readers and audiences, as say a western, a film noir, a detective story or a situation comedy. 'The function of genre conventions is essentially to establish a contract between writer and reader so as to make certain relevant expectations operative and thus to permit both compliance with and deviation from accepted modes of intelligibility' (Culler, 1975: 147). The fourth is most easily expressed as a kind of second-order naturalization or reflexivity in which texts refer to themselves as artificial but, as a result, in that self-knowledge, reclaim their authenticity. The audible and self-conscious narrator is one expression of this version of *vraisemblance*: the setting of television news in a working newsroom might be another. The final dimension is that of intertextuality; through parody, irony, pastiche and simply through reference to other content or form, texts refer to each other and in so doing claim a certain kind of naturalness, a familiarity upon which to build their difference and their surprise.

All of these are textual strategies, but like rhetoric, they are claims not commitments. We can resist the blandishments of even a well-turned plot. We can convert its message into our own. And of course we do. All the time. Much research has been conducted within the study of the media over recent years which insists on the capacity of readers and audiences to make their own meanings when confronted with the singular text. *Dallas* was a significant focus, and justifiably, not just because of its huge US audiences but because of its global appeal, with the exception of Japan, that is. Studies here drew out the particular characteristics of audiences' relationships to *Dallas* as a story, seeing it as a focus of sentimental attachment in which viewers engaged and identified with situations rather than with the realism of the non-realistic plot (Ang, 1986), or with the capacity of ethnically distinct audiences to relate their own lives to the narrative through identification with moral, political and economic dilemmas (Liebes and Katz, 1990). Each of these studies, and there are many others, links textual representation to experience, or at least some aspect of experience, without perhaps addressing experience as such.

Trust is a negotiable commodity here as elsewhere in the process of mediation. And experience? Let us not reify it. We still need to understand how media enter into the worlds of everyday life, how their poetry reaches and touches and enables us to make sense and manage and get on. It is in this sense that a poetics of the media must interpret the requirement to identify 'the general laws that preside over the birth of each work' to include the making of meanings beyond the point of the work's publication, for these, in their attenuation, are rule governed too (if not law-like); subject as they are to the structured patterns of social life. Indeed, Aristotle's *Poetics* does not speak of structure but of structuration, and, as I have already insisted, structuration (or in my terms *mediation*) is only completed in the mind or the life of the reader or viewer.

There are links to be made between narrative and practical understanding. 'If, in fact, human action can be narrated, it is because it is always already articulated by signs, rules and norms. It is always already symbolically mediated . . . symbolic forms are cultural processes that articulate experience.' Thus Paul Ricoeur (1984: 57), discussing the relationship between time and narrative, and drawing on Augustine and Aristotle (as well as, in this quotation, Ernst Cassirer), places, as I have already begun to do, mimesis as the key link between narrative and experience. And for Ricoeur time is of the essence. It is the temporal ordering of experience which allows us to follow the temporal ordering of a narrative, and it is the temporal ordering of narrative which allows us to make sense of experience; 'time becomes human to the extent that it is articulated through a narrative mode, and narrative attains its full meaning when it becomes a condition of temporal existence' (Ricoeur, 1984: 52).

I can follow a story because I live in time. I have my beginning and my ending, once and finally, but also multiply in the hours and days and years of my shared life with others. That life is suffused with narratives, both public and private, narratives which enable me to make sense, some sense at least, of who and what and where I am. The stories I listen to, the ones I repeat or imagine, are based on my experiences of time, and those experiences are themselves dependent on my knowledge of those stories.

Our media exist in time: the time of the annual calendar of great events, themselves narrated in time; the time of the weekly and daily schedule, modelled on and reinforcing the temporality of the working week; the time of the interrupted narratives of news and soap opera; the time of the endlessly recursive confessions of day-time talk shows, narrative upon narrative, beginnings and middle and ends, stories to repeat, to remember to reject and resist. Such narratives explain. They tell us how it is; and it *is* how they tell us, not just in the subjunctive fantasies of the 'as-if', but through our capacity to recognize ourselves, somewhere, some of the time, within them. And following a plot involves engagement in different qualities of time; in its configuration, its wholeness, in the sense of its ending, in the recognition of the familiar and, in repetition, an expression of the non-linear, the non-progressive. Time forward and time reverse. Time repeated. Time interrupted. Fast. Slow. Lines and circles. The framing and the framed. It is biological and social time which informs our capacity to read and to listen, and it is biological and social time, arguably, which underlies the capacity of media tales, some of them, to ignore the specificity of cultures.

Just as in my consideration of rhetoric I had to distinguish between mystery and mystification and to require that a media rhetoric enquire into both, into their interrelationship and the implications of their contradictions, so too now. As Elin Diamond reminds us, we need to differentiate between mimesis and mimicry, and to remember, as she does, how powerfully distrusting was Plato's account of the image. The mirror lies. But worse than that, it seduces its holder into believing that the power of the real is captured in its image. For Diamond the mirror is an enabling tool, and a gendered one at that; not for fidelity, but for difference, not for reflection but refraction, and mimesis is not a matter of imitation but representation. Mimesis is performance. Mimesis, like performance, 'is a doing and a thing done'. And so it is. Mimesis *is* enabling. It is not necessarily true. 'On the one hand [mimesis] speaks to our desire for universality, coherence, unity, tradition, and on the other, it unravels that unity through improvisation, embodied rhythm, powerful instantiations of subjectivity, and what Plato most dreaded . . . mimicry' (Diamond, 1997: v).

Our media poetics has therefore to go beyond the descriptive. It cannot take the face value at face value. Yet it must understand that critique depends on an understanding of the processes at work. Our delight in stories, our capacity to relax beside them, to give up something of the pressures of daily life beside the loud speaker or in front of the screen, are part of what it is that enables us to remain human. This is not mere sentiment. That capacity, that ability to suspend disbelief, to enter the barely bounded territory of the 'as-if' in search of the pleasures of cognition and recognition, is probably as important now, if not more so, than it has ever been. Yet the consequences of that engagement, for identity and culture, for our capacity to continue to act *in* the world, are still far from understood.

This argument has its own consequences in turn. It needs to be remembered before we run fearfully to lay the disasters of contemporary immorality or criminality at the door of the media, as if coincidence were causation, as if juxtaposition were explanation, as if the stories of unmediated influence were mirrors, as if our actions were not themselves influences and frameworks for understanding, as if the storyteller were somehow removed from the society in which she tells her stories. As if.

6 Erotics

Pleasure is a problem, of course. Not for us as individuals maybe. We know what we like, what turns us on. Our tastes are clear enough. We seek out sensation; in our modest ways. Pleasures shared or pleasures guilty. We turn to the programmes or the web-sites that we think will please us, seeking to recover yesterday's buzz, yesterday's fun. Pleasure in the game, the joke, the situation, the fantasy. Nothing wrong in that. Innocent. Entertainment. No harm to anyone.

The media industries are geared to making pleasure come, easy and eternal. Naturally. Our own private Xanadus. The CDs piled high in a corner of the room, the videos in the cupboard, the favourite sites a click away; and pleasures to be taken on the move; inside the home and outside it, televisually, cinematically, plugged in to walkmen and to hi-fis.

In this chapter I want to discuss the erotic not so much as a product of the text but as a product of the relationship between viewers, readers and audiences and the texts and media events that offer pleasure. Pleasure requires participation. The balance of power shifts towards the consumer. Pleasures of the body and pleasures of the mind; the physical and cerebral intertwined. Pleasure, excitement, sensation, these are constantly offered, but not often really delivered; unconsummation is the norm.

Yes, pleasure is a problem in many ways. We know what we like but will find it difficult to explain why we like what we do. We spend a lot of time in front of the television set watching our favourite programmes, but yet we often feel less than satisfied with the result. We are being told by the cultural policemen of left and right that the pleasures to be gained from media culture are either undermining or false: that they trivialize, distort; they seduce us from the real world. And we are told by moral minorities that some pleasures are entirely wrong: that the pleasures to be had from sex and violence should neither be offered nor accepted. Yet in a world increasingly based on an ideology of the individual's right to consume, there are plenty of voices to defend and legitimate any pleasure and the media's rights to give people what they want.

There are yet deeper problems, for us, as we study the media. For our thinking is still constrained, even in a post-Cartesian world, by the separation of mind and body, and by the priority given to the definition of the human as a rational creature. As a result we can think about thinking well enough, but feeling is altogether another story. Sensation, significance, desire, these are things we neither discuss much in our everyday lives nor in our theories. The erotic escapes. Shame and reason conspire to repress it. The body disappears behind the curtain of the mind.

In 1939 a Penguin Special, *Britain*, by Mass Observation, appeared in the bookshops of the United Kingdom. As the cover of that first edition records, 'Mass-observation, a movement started early in 1937 by two young men and now embracing some two thousand voluntary observers all over the country, exists to study everyday behaviour in Britain – the Science of Ourselves.' It was a kind of spontaneous sociology. Charles Madge and Tom Harrisson set out to investigate and to record what the nation was really thinking. At a time when politicians in their attempts both to mobilize support and to legitimate their own indecisiveness would keep referring to what the nation wants and believes and thinks, these two young men decided to investigate what the nation really did want and believe and think. It was, it might be said, the beginnings of public opinion research in this country, but it was also the beginnings of an attempt, in which we are still engaged, to go behind the public pronouncements of ideology and policy and to listen to the voices of ordinary folk whose lives and whose agendas would, without such investigation, be invisible, taken for granted and too easily exploitable.

It is a wonderful, surreal, book. Their investigation involved enquiring into what folk believed and understood about the gathering storm in general and Chamberlain's moves to defuse it in particular. Crisis. What crisis? It was a test of knowledge and it was test of belief, but it was not just about politics. For Madge and Harrisson percipiently recognized that the everyday had its own culture, and that this popular, pretty much exclusively working-class, culture, and the values that informed it, were as legitimate as any other. There was life there. It was different. And it was physical.

We can put to one side for a moment the charge that the study itself reinforced a kind of Lawrentian romanticization of the earthy working classes, as we follow their account into their vitality. Instead we can focus on the voices of the respondents, their defence on the pages of the book and the slightly quizzical, slightly perplexed, distance that separates the observers and the observed.

One study was based around the Lambeth Walk, the popular, and briefly global, dance craze of the time (in October of 1938 a 'brunette' went to Rome to teach it to Mussolini, and 'Mayfair's socialite sportsman, Russian Prince Sergei Obolonsky introduced it to New York café society on July 29th'). The Lambeth Walk had its origins, literally, in the strutting of the male working-class Cockney *flâneur* and it returned to urban dance floors via its appropriation severally by Noel Gay, the Cambridge-educated composer of the show *Me and My Girl*, of which it was the hit song, Lupino Lane, the music-hall comedian who became its star, Mr C. L. Heimann, managing director of the Locarno dance halls, and Miss Adèle England, principal dancer at their Streatham branch, who between them created and demonstrated the new dance and its steps. Not to mention the BBC who broadcast the song intensively. Pursuing the origins of the dance, Madge and Harrisson discovered an underbelly of working-class culture: of spontaneous parties, of cross-dressing and physical excess. As one observer himself notes, comparing his experience of the Lambeth Walk with native dances of Southern Sudan: 'They finish up quite frankly in the way one might expect. In my view eroticism is the main attraction of all dancing' (retired major, Mass Observation, 1939: 171).

A second study was of all-in wrestling, that sport which has now been consigned to the margins of cable television, having had its brief flowering in the UK at least in the early years of commercial television, but which was very much the vogue in live venues in the working-class cities of northern England before the war. Madge and Harrisson talked to the promoters and to the wrestlers, but above all they talked to the punters. They talked about a sport that was not quite a sport. It was professional and above all it was performance. These were the gladiators. Forcing it. Faking it. Playing to the crowd. Mass media before television. What were its pleasures? They were erotic. Here are two of the voices:

> Almost every wrestler is an individualist. They are not encumbered by lots of rules and fine points such as is the case in boxing . . . therefore each wrestler develops a style and many tricks and gestures that are essentially his own. Secondly like those unusual incidents that are absent in other sports. Such as German wrestler giving the Nazi salute and getting the raspberry in return. Ali Baba taking out his mat and praying to Allah. Wrestlers refusing to fight until their opponent's nails have been cut or grease wiped off his back, this latter act causing intense excitement before the fight has commenced. Smashing the bowl on each other's head, breaking the stool, challenging and spitting on the audience, dancing, shouting and running across the ring in a temper, tearing the referee's shirt off, jumping on it and then throwing the referee out of the ring. (a regular, Mass Observation, 1939: 132–3)

> Wrestling at first disgusted me, but now I like it very much. No other sport has such fine husky specimens of manhood as wrestling. I find it such a change to see real he men after the spineless and insipid men one meets ordinarily. (a woman, Mass Observation, 1939: 133)

Forbidden pleasures? Not quite, but certainly ones that are unlikely to be acknowledged within middle-class culture, and certainly not in 1938. For this is body talk.

Yet we all have our moments, those moments, even on the screen, when the raw and physical excitement of life, of the live, the explosion of strength or skill or beauty transcends the normal and placid routine pleasures of media consumption and bursts unannounced, but always desired and anticipated, on to our senses. The moment when Scott Hastings, Scottish full-back and captain, bursts through the French lines at the end of a losing rugby match at the Parc des Princes and thunders towards the touch line and the camera placed there to capture just this moment: muscles pulsing, cheeks pumping, sinews stretched, no other thought possible. Or Bruce Springsteen, or Tom Jones. Sport and music. Performance and play. Such moments are transcendent, the sublime of mediated as well as non-mediated culture, but dependent both, pretty much, on the live or the manifest representation of the live; and dependent too on the conjunction of sound and image and surprise, and physical commitment. Action replays are no substitute for the goal. It has to be real.

Eros is life. The connection is incontestable. The live becomes life when the body is touched. The gasp of recognition, identification, surprise, and the groan of pleasure. Freud in his later work saw in Eros the foundation of civilization, as well as in the tension between life and death, its motor. We too are coming to see how important bodies are to an understanding of society and culture, and I have already suggested the centrality of the body both to experience and to our capacity to share it.

But how do media texts connect to bodies? How do they claim us as erotic subjects? In many ways, of course. In many, many ways. Mass Observation constructs its accounts of mediated pleasures through the unself-conscious observations of participants, through a framework significantly influenced both by surrealism and psychoanalysis. Other accounts are more personal, enquiring into the particular erotic threads that weave the spell that fixes and transfixes. The sting. In pursuing this way of thinking about the erotic I want to engage the ideas of one of its supreme theorists, not so much to endorse but to illustrate what can be thought and said. There is space for this on the agenda of those who wish to study the media, difficult though it may be to know quite how to work with the issues that are raised.

Here, then, is Roland Barthes, the great literary critic and supreme theorist of the textual sublime:

> Is not the most erotic portion of the body *where the garment gapes?* In perversion (which is the realm of textual pleasure) there are no 'erogenous zones' . . . it is intermittence, as psychoanalysis has so rightly stated, which is erotic; the intermittence of skin flashing between two articles of clothing (trousers and sweater), between two edges (the open-necked shirt, the glove

> and the sleeve); it is this flash which seduces, or rather: the staging of an appearance-as-disappearance. (Barthes, 1976: 9–10)

Barthes rejects the claimed eroticism of the cumulative striptease of narrative, defining exquisite pleasure as that which comes from the breaking free from the constructed, comfortable, expected pleasures of reading, or watching. The contrast is indeed between pleasure and bliss (*jouissance* in French). Whereas the former reinforces, the latter unsettles. It is the question which is erotic, not the answer. Barthes, one will not be surprised to discover, does not find much genuinely erotic in the products of mass culture. In their repetition, in their exploitation of the presumed pleasures that their audiences will seek and inevitably find, in the fetishizing of the new; in the control these texts claim and indeed exercise over the reader, there is nothing much there for him. There are books that prompt desire, constructing and anticipating pleasures to come, and which will, inevitably, disappoint, as all desire is bound to be disappointed; and there are books which provide those moments of *jouissance*: 'the moment when my body pursues its own ideas – for my body does not have the same ideas as I do' (Barthes, 1976: 17).

This discussion is personal without being subjective. Barthes asks us to consider, through his own experience, and his own both implicit and explicit declaration in this and other texts of his own sexuality, our own position in relation to the things we read and see; the things we seek for our pleasures, and the things which transcend those expected pleasures. We need not confine our own version of the erotic to Barthes's, but we each do *have* our own version. And if we feel uncomfortable with the discourse, then that's how it has to be, for the erotic is difficult. We do not have a language for it; indeed, it does of its very nature escape language.

I want, nevertheless, to stay with Barthes a moment longer, for in his last major book, *Camera Lucida* (1981), he pursues these issues again, though this time in the context of the photographic image rather than the word. And as he does so he draws us closer, too, to the world of electronic media.

In his preoccupation with the image, the terms *plaisir* and *jouissance* are replaced by two others, this time drawn from classical language and theory. He is looking at a photograph. What does he see? He sees two things. He sees an image. He sees what that image has captured: what the photographer may have intended in taking it and framing it as a cultural object. The image interests him. He respects it. He notes how familiar it is, even though he may never have seen it before. He sees, indeed, in all photographs, death: an image, a moment, a person, who no longer is, who is no longer quite like that. He recognizes the fidelity of the image even though he knows that it is constructed. He knows that even though a photograph is condemned by the time and the place of its taking, and its own partiality, it nevertheless tells the truth. This *is* how it *was*. The camera cannot lie: 'The photograph then becomes a bizarre medium, a new form of hallucination: false on the level of perception, true on the level of time: a temporal hallucination . . . (on the one hand "it is not there", on the other "but it has indeed been")' (Barthes, 1981: 115). The photograph naturalizes its own bizarreness. And we are comfortable with the generality of it. This general sense of seeing, this general claim for a photograph to be seen, Barthes calls the *studium*.

But Barthes also sees something else in the photograph, or at least in some photographs. He calls this the *punctum*. It is the prick of the unexpected. Something in the image which fractures it, an accident, a moment, a point, which in his inimitable words 'bruises me, is poignant to me' (Barthes, 1981: 27). Whereas the *studium* is coded – it fits into the rules of framing and expectation, it guarantees the photograph as readable and the image as recognizable – the *punctum* is not. And once again the *punctum* is that which escapes, albeit momentarily, language. I might not even see it at first, but it lives in me and in my recognition of its significance (I have to become Barthes at this moment), and like the transitional object that Winnicott argues is the seed of creativity, Barthes sees the *punctum* as an addition: 'it is what I add to the photograph and *what is nonetheless already there*' (Barthes, 1981: 55, italics in original).

So what does he see? A sense of Victorian-ness in a photograph of Queen Victoria on a horse with John Brown at her side. The tenderness of a hand (Mapplethorpe's) on an outstretched arm in an image of a head and partial torso; a glimpse into the private world of childhood in a cloth cap on a Russian child; the claim of respectability in the strapped pumps worn by a black woman in a family portrait: the detail, the unexpected, the pregnant; that which bursts upon a viewer and bursts through the frame offering significance, which is, as he says, 'meaning, *insofar as it is sensually produced*' (Barthes, 1976: 61, italics in original).

The *punctum* eroticizes the image, in Barthes's view, and eroticizes the relationship between viewer and image. Just as it is the fracture in the written text which touches him, so too here it is the prick in the visual: a synaesthetic moment of pure pleasure, and which in both word and image involves the fizzing conjunction between the body written and seen with the body reading and seeing.

There are dangers in pursuing this too far. Yet there is still more to be said, for Barthes, suspicious as he is of the premeditated in all its textual forms, nevertheless hazards a number of observations on the news photograph, on cinema, and on pornography, which will allow me to move beyond the specific nature of his formulization of the erotic and at the same time to make the case for the significance *of* the erotic as a key to understanding how our media work. Doing so will in turn require a modest reading of him against the grain.

To start with. News photographs are not erotic:

> In these images, no *punctum*: a certain shock – the literal can traumatise – but no disturbance; the photograph can 'shout', not wound. These journalistic photographs are received (all at once), perceived. I glance through them, I don't recall them; no detail (in some corner) ever interrupts my reading: I am interested in them (as I am interested in the world), I do not love them. (Barthes, 1981: 41)

News photographs, and he has already analysed them in their mythic and ideological manifestations in an earlier work (Barthes, 1972), are all *studium*. The images that they contain are unitary (he calls them unary): a single message, a single meaning is all that is claimed, all that is required. Reality represented without irony and without disturbance. Two things might follow from this. The first is, perhaps, a way towards understanding why it is that images of violence in the news are never seen as cause for censure; it is because, in their integrity, they do not provoke; they are asexual. The second is quite different. It is to say that notwithstanding Barthes's own preferences and his antipathy to the generality of the news image, it is perfectly possible to imagine that such an image *could* be eroticized by another reader, a not-Barthes. Just as rhetoric and poetics requires the presence of the reader or the auditor, so too now. Here, as elsewhere, it takes two to tango.

And likewise the cinema. Barthes is drawn to it negatively, as it were, as undermining the possibility of an erotic touch. For the cinema is in motion, and the image is never still enough. It is drawn ever onwards, a flow which carries with it an immediate recollection of what has just passed and an anticipation of what will come. The cinematic image does:

> not cling to me. . . . Like the real world, the filmic world is sustained by the presumption that, as Husserl says, 'experience will constantly continue to flow by in the same constitutive style'; but the Photograph breaks the 'constitutive style' (this is its astonishment); it is *without future* (this is its pathos, its melancholy). . . . (Barthes, 1981: 90)

It is the flow that kills: something we might also observe in television (but not yet necessarily on the web). Yet maybe too we know better than this. Perhaps we have, on the other hand, learned how the cinema and the cinematic gaze, that is the way in which we can and do look at ourselves in the mirror of the filmic image, is still in some significant way erotic, albeit, as many have suggested, narcissistic, auto-erotic.

And, finally, to the pornographic: the torn corner of media's erotic life and our erotic life with our media. It goes without saying that pornography is a pure commodity, it exploits; indeed, it is exploitation personified; capitalism at its most intense, in its most naked form. But it is not, in Barthes's view, necessarily, or even ever, erotic. Pornography's representation of the sexual organs makes them into 'a motionless object (a fetish), flattered like an idol that does not leave its niche . . . there is no *punctum* in the pornographic image . . . the pornographic body shows itself, it does not give itself, there is no generosity in it' (Barthes, 1981: 59).

We are being driven towards the audience. The erotic is, in the beginning and the end of it, in the person. Texts, as I have observed, can do no more than claim. And Barthes too makes his claims. His is one voice among many. But what he signals is the exquisite power of the text: the capacity of the written word or the mediated image to capture the moment, to touch, to inspire, to seduce. Of course, researchers in the field have for years been preoccupied with the effects of the media on those who read or watch, effects which have from to time been measured in laboratories through techniques that monitor sexual arousal. Others, similarly preoccupied, have called on arguably more natural methodologies in their attempt to discover the sources of media power: interviews, observations, ethnographies of everyday life. And yet others have taken the psychoanalytic route, one indeed that both Barthes and I too, in this chapter, have drawn upon, to explore the hidden and the inexpressible in desire as a way of connecting people, their passions and their media preferences. Each of these in their various ways is an attempt to understand how the media work, and of course how we work with the media. Each is an attempt to understand significance.

But Barthes also suggests, despite himself, something else. There is bliss in mass culture. The erotic is both a precondition of experience and its justification. We are drawn to these otherwise mundane and trivial texts and performances by a transcendent hope, a hope and a desire that something will touch us. And we look, and on occasion find, something that goes beyond the merely suggestive. We go back, too, to those sites and those programmes where we have found it once and hope to do so again. Our obsessions, with soap operas or football games or slasher movies or with film stars and music videos, are ways of maximizing our chances. Yet, and it is in the nature of such things, such searches are so often entirely self-defeating. Goalless draws.

It is difficult, of course, to engage in the discussion of such issues without making one's own value judgements, without imposing one's own taste, one's own versions of what counts as erotic, authentic, real. It is difficult, too, to avoid reflecting on how our culture, in its own sophistication, embodies what it takes to be the erotic and plasters it on the walls and screens and pages of public life. How the erotic becomes the sexy, and how the sexy is all that it seems to take. It is difficult to avoid assertions of pathology, both in relation to the individual and to society as a whole.

It is, indeed, a commonplace to observe that everything is reducible to sex. Psychoanalysis's own obsession has been trivialized and distorted in the telling and in its own mechanical reproduction. My point here is a different one. I have been at pains to identify an enquiry into that part of our lives which escapes easy acknowledgement; to confront, however inadequately, the force of the non-rational in everyday life and as a component of our media consumption. I wish to recognize disturbance and grant it its place. I have been seeking the unconscious in the hidden meanings of minds, media and experience. I have done no more, in this chapter especially, than open a window. It is one, however, that should not be closed.

Dimensions of experience

The new, now classic, question asked by those working on media research in the 1950s and 1960s was not 'ask what the media do to us', but 'ask what we do with our media'. This is my question now, though it has to be reframed. In this section I intend to enquire more deeply into the ways in which media texts, the technologies that deliver them and our own responses to what we see, hear and with which we interact, themselves interact. What are the mechanisms of engagement? How are we to understand the social and cultural dimensions of mediation as they emerge at the point of connection with our media? What aspects of experience intersect with the images, voices and sounds that comprise our media environment?

In the intertwining of media's meanings with our own, we are neither free nor in chains. Nor do we anymore engage, even if we ever did, with the products of the media in a rational or functional way. The spaces we live in, in our inner as well as our outer worlds, are complicated by the lives we lead and the press of media on our minds and souls. Boundaries are there to be broken. Sounds to be remastered. Images to be refashioned. But meanings are there to be fixed, accepted, owned, if only for the moment. The press of information, its noise, its intrusion. The endless demands to choose, to decipher, to discriminate. What do we do with our media and how do we do it? How do we manage?

The study of the media involves enquiry into the social psychology and sociology of the viewing experience and the experience of viewing, which is not the same thing. It requires an investigation into the spaces that form around and beyond the interface: eyeball, ear-drum, screen and speaker. These spaces are discursive. Within them meanings are made and rejected. The presumption is that, in some sense, the television viewer or radio listener (and not just the newspaper *reader*) is active; that viewing and listening and reading require some degree of commitment, some kind of choices, some type of consequence. The presumption is that we come to our media as sentient beings (notwithstanding the empty cans of lager cluttered around the settee after a night in front of the box). And the presumption is that the meanings we make that involve our media, that may require or depend upon them, are meanings like any other and the product of our capacity, as social beings, to be in the world.

In this section I explore some ways of thinking about this problem of meaning-making and experience. The exploration involves an enquiry into the different kinds of relationships we have with our media. It involves an understanding of both media and their audiences as players, representing one to the other, making claims and counter-claims, asking each other questions, sharing a context for action in which both, in different degrees, in different ways and at different times, are agents. This context for action is associated with rhetoric's commonplace, and poetic's mimesis. It is where media meet everyday life.

7 Play

The media experience is, in some significant and general sense, as I have begun to suggest, subjunctive. To be in the world but not of it. To be of it but not in it. To see the media as providing a frame for experience, but also to see the media themselves as being transformed by experience. To recognize the media's role in contributing to the different timbres and hues of everyday life; to its ordinariness as well as to its uniqueness; to both the generality of experience and to the intensity of *the* experience: those seminal, structural events that are, both for individuals and groups, decisive in defining identity and culture. To acknowledge that so much of culture, our culture, our media culture, consists in the acceptance of the 'as-if-ness' of the world.

Everyday life involves continuous movement across boundaries and thresholds: between the public and private; between the sacred and the profane; between front and back stages; between the realms of the real and the fantastic; between inner and outer reality, the individual and the social. Some of these boundaries are quite indistinct, invisible to the naked eye, insignificant. Others are more clearly marked: marked by the events, both mediated and unmediated, that stud everyday life and provide the occasion for different kinds of, or particularly intense, social action. It can, of course, be argued that in our late modern, or even post-modern, world such boundaries are indeed increasingly becoming indistinct, as realities blur or are homogenized, as much as anything as a result of the media themselves, and as the highly ritualized pre-modern or modernizing societies give way to a new social and cultural order. Yet it can also be argued that, weaker or not, these boundaries and thresholds still exist, and that they are daily recreated in the activities and lives of both urban and suburban folk, in popular and sub-cultures as well as in high culture, and in the endless avoidance or engagement rituals of the daily round.

Many writers, both in the social and the human sciences, have addressed these questions and have found in the notion of *play* a powerful way of investigating them. I want in this chapter to explore play as a tool for the analysis of the media experience, and to suggest that the study of the media requires attention to play as a core activity of daily life, though one mostly overlooked especially in Enlightenment or post-Enlightenment discourses which insist on, and only value, sober rationality and the increasing and appropriate disenchantment of the world. This is not, of course, to suggest that play is irrational, and that the games that institutionalize play in the modern world are themselves the focus of, and for, non-rational action. On the contrary, play is entirely rational. It is just that its forms of rationality are not those of the mundane, the quotidian. Well, not quite. Play is part of everyday life, just as it is separate from it. To step into a space and a time to play is to move across a threshold, to leave something behind – one kind of order – and to grasp a different reality and a rationality defined by its own rules and terms of trade and action. We play to leave the world. But it is not the world. And we return.

Play is a space in which meanings are constructed through participation within a shared and structured place, a place ritually demarcated as being distinct from, and other than, the ordinariness of everyday life, a place of modest security and trust, in which players can safely leave real life and engage in an activity that is meaningful in its rule-governed excess. As Jan Huizinga (1970) defines it:

> play is a voluntary activity. Play to order is no longer play. . . . A second characteristic is closely connected with this, namely, that play is not 'ordinary' or 'real' life. It is rather a stepping out of 'real' life into a temporary sphere of activity with a disposition all of its own. . . . As regards its formal characteristics, all students lay stress on the *disinterestedness* of play. Not being 'ordinary' life it stands outside the immediate satisfaction of wants and appetites. . . . Play is distinct from 'ordinary' life both as to locality and duration. This is the third main characteristic of play: its secludedness, its limitedness . . . [play] creates order, *is* order. . . . All play has its rules. They determine what 'holds' in the temporary world circumscribed by play. (Huizinga, 1970: 26–30)

For Huizinga play involves, both literally and metaphorically, a bounded space. Play is the general category of which games are the specific embodiment. The notion of play both exceeds and contains the game. Play is associated with ritual, and ritual, as we shall see in the next chapter, is also linked to performance. Play involves the suspension of disbelief, not 'complete illusion' (Huizinga, 1970: 41). Play is 'as-if' culture *par excellence*.

There are many ways in which we can see the media as being sites for play, both in their texts and in the responses that those texts engender. And not just in the endless thud of the computer game. Watching television, surfing the net, doing the crossword, guessing the answers in a

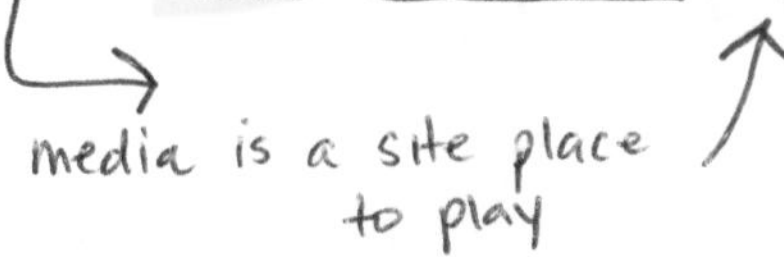

quiz, taking part in a lottery, all involve play. The media have the capacity, indeed they entirely depend upon that capacity, to engage an audience within spaces and times that are distinguished – marked off – from the otherwise relentless confusions of everyday life. There is a threshold to be crossed each time we participate in the process of mediation. New freedoms but also new rules. New pleasures. Both surprises and security. The challenge of the new within the bounds of the familiar. Risks managed. Games, in their endless, electronic recurrence, that, unlike in life, we never really lose.

Roger Caillois (1962) has both developed and offered a critique of Huizinga. He too describes play as essentially free, circumscribed within limits of time and space, uncertain, unproductive, governed by rules under conventions that suspend ordinary laws, and involving make believe. It is 'accompanied by a special awareness of a second reality or of a free unreality, as against real life' (Caillois, 1962: 10). And he goes on to distinguish four dimensions of play: beginning with *agon* (competitiveness) and *alea* (chance):

> *Agon* and *alea* imply opposite and somewhat complementary attitudes, but they both obey the same law – the creation for the players of conditions of pure equality denied them in real life. For nothing in life is clear. . . . Play, whether *agon* or *alea* is thus an attempt to substitute perfect situations for the normal confusion of contemporary life. (Caillois, 1962: 19)

And then moving on to *ilinx* (vertigo, surrender, possession of a physical kind) and *mimicry* (masquerade and identification, pleasure in passing for another):

> With one exception, *mimicry* exhibits all the characteristics of play: liberty, convention, suspension of reality, and delimitation of space and time. However, the continuous submission to imperative and precise rules cannot be observed – rules for the dissimulation of reality and the substitution of a second reality. *Mimicry* is incessant invention. The rule of the game is unique: it consists in the actor's fascinating the spectator, while avoiding an error that might lead the spectator to break the spell. The spectator must lend himself to the illusion without first challenging the décor, mask, or artifice which for a given time he is asked to believe in as more real than reality itself. (Caillois, 1958: 23)

Here is mimicry as mimetic performance, and here too a link between the ludic and the dramatic. The play's the thing.

Caillois also distinguished between those kinds of activities that emphasize spontaneity and improvisation (*paidia*) and those that are significantly rule governed (*ludus*), a continuum leading from play to (civilizing) games. *Paidia*, as its name implies, is associated with childhood play and

improvised games. *Ludus* suggests 'the specific element in play the impact and cultural creativity of which seems most impressive. It does not connote a psychological attitude as precise as that of *agon*, *alea*, *mimicry* or *ilinx*, but in disciplining the *paidia*, its general contribution is to give the fundamental categories of play their purity and excellence' (Caillois, 1962: 33).

The approach is at once sociological and normative. Within an emergent anthropology and history of play Caillois nevertheless expresses his own fear of the conjunction of *mimicry* and *ilinx*, detecting, perhaps unsurprisingly in the aftermath of world war and fascist excess, their dangers in public spaces and their revival in modern society. Yet he notes, with approval, their constructive disjunction: in carnival, travelling fairs and the circus. What he would think of our electronic media is another matter entirely.

Popular culture has therefore always been a playful culture. It has taken the serious and often oppressive regulation of the conduct of everyday life, the regulation by state, religion and community, and turned it on its head: carnival, bacchanalia, charivari. The lords of misrule held sway over the cracks in the dominant, offering the oppressed and the routinized the momentary licence of public play and display. At such times and in such spaces, both physically and symbolically expressed and marked by thresholds within experience, individuals and groups could suspend the regularities of the daily, take pleasure and, in some transcendent way, play with the categories and concepts of the world over which they otherwise had no influence. I return to this theme in Chapter 11.

Such play was escape but also connection. Life was left, if only for the moment, but that world remained inscribed but transformed in the topsy-turvy games of social discord and resistance. The transitions were crucial. The meanings generated outlived the moment of their experience. The calendar was marked by the regularities of their occurrence. They were always a threat. The crowd. The mob. The pagan. The popular. Yet, as Peter Burke (1978) has so brilliantly documented, the relationships between popular and high culture were never quite so distinct. Elites, too, had their moments, in masque and through jester; though licenced as they were by high society as well as high culture, *they* needed, as it were, no other source of legitimation. And indeed, the two social divisions learned from each other and, in one way or another, both provided for, and depended on, each other.

In our world of electronic media we can recognize the same playfulness, the same marked spaces and times for amusement, though the boundaries between play and seriousness are more permeable and less distinct these days. Still, we play. And we play with and through our media. We play with and around them, as we watch and engage, with more or less pleasure, in the gladiatorial trials of the televised football game or the manufactured romance of the televised dating game. We watch our society being re*played* in the recursive narratives of soap opera. We play on the net, downloading games, role-taking, role-making with other players, players not known to us except through the characters they take, as allies and opponents in electronic space. Play masters and mistresses in virtual dungeons. We take pleasure, too, in the scurrilous and the seditious: in the sophistication of the satirical, but also in the pages of the tabloid press: not news, not a *news*paper. Of course not. Fun though. And we dance, some of us at least, to the drum and bass of ecstatic rituals. Clubbing, playing, and, of course, performing too.

Contained and limited though they arguably might be seen to be, these moments and sites for play allow and legitimate a modicum of re-enchantment in our otherwise disenchanted lives. How we come to value these moments, and how we come to assess their worth and consequences in their various expressions across and within cultures is still an issue, and I'll come to that. But to pretend that such re-enchantment does not exist or that it has no value, or to deny that play might be constructive, that mimicry might be educative, and that games might be cathartic both for players and audiences, seems to me to miss an essential dimension of social life.

Play is central, or so it seems, to media experience. We find its source both in the specifics of genre and programming and in the activities of viewing and listening. Play involves, like rhetoric, mutual participation. Players and their audiences, and audiences who become, even at one remove, players, together are involved in discourses which the media claim and construct and which punctuate, and puncture, our daily lives.

However it is important to note, as Caillois does particularly, the tensions identified in play and games between 'contained freedom', 'secure creativity', 'active passivity', 'voluntary dependence'. There is nothing simple to be found either in the sociology or anthropology of play, or in its mediation. Indeed digging deeper produces a sense of a more complex, psychodynamic reality, and one which relates play as an activity both to the construction of an individual's identity and to the mechanics of culture as a process and an achievement. Play is both a complex and a precarious activity.

Its precariousness is recognized by the British psychoanalyst D.W. Winnicott in his discussion of the relationship between playing and reality:

> Play is immensely exciting. It is exciting not because the instincts are involved, *be it understood!* The thing about playing is always the precariousness of the

> interplay of personal psychic reality and the experience of control of actual objects. This is the precariousness of magic itself, magic that arises in intimacy, in a relationship that is being found to be reliable. (Winnicott, 1974: 55)

Winnicott places play at the centre of his psychology of childhood. His approach is based on the analysis of the pre-linguistic child and his or her object relations, principally and initially with the mother, and then in a process of separation and individuation with transitional objects which become the site of fantasy and the negotiation of illusion and disillusion. Here too play occupies a space, both literally and metaphorically, in which the trusting child explores the world through the manipulation of objects and the construction of fantasy. Through play, and within an environment which offers trust and security and in which play can be both stimulated and contained, a child pleasurably constructs for herself or himself a place in culture. Play occupies and depends upon a transitional space, transitional between the inner world and that of external reality in which, as it might be, both can be tested against one another in a creative way. This is what the child does, argues Winnicott, in the manipulation of objects: playing is being and playing is doing. External reality is tested; internal reality is defined, gradually, through such testing and through the near-hallucination that play requires. And through such testing, such play, the child constructs a symbolic world, a world of meanings and securities: a private but also a public culture.

So for Winnicott play is the activity in which the child begins, creatively, to explore the boundary between self and other, between the inside and outside:

> To get to the idea of playing it is helpful to think of the *preoccupation* that characterises the playing of a young child. The content does not matter. What matters is the near-withdrawal state, akin to the *concentration* of older children and adults. The playing child inhabits an area that cannot be easily left, nor can it easily admit intrusions. . . . This area of playing is not inner psychic reality. It is outside the individual, but it is not the external world. (Winnicott, 1974: 60)

The tensions which Caillois identifies anthropologically are here revealed in their psychodynamic underpinnings. Play brings the child out in the adult; and the adult out in the child. Play enables the exploration of that tissue boundary between fantasy and reality, between the real and the imagined, between the self and the other. In play we have a licence to explore, both our selves and our society. In play we investigate culture, but we also create it. There is safety in this but also danger, since boundaries cannot always be held, and the trust we require may not always be offered. We act but we also act out. We make mistakes. We get stuck. We misread the signs. And sometimes tragically so.

But there is pleasure in it. The pleasure of the game well played, the move well made, the chance well taken, the risk well run, the challenge well met, the guess well made, the dream fulfilled. There is pleasure in participation. In the partnership and in the rivalry. In observation. In identification. In sublimation. In regression. In playing and in playfulness.

It has been said of the electronic media, and of the age defined by their dominance, that the boundaries which have hitherto been sacred are now transgressed: both social boundaries, between the child and the adult or between female and male, and symbolic boundaries, between reality and fantasy, between the serious and the less than serious. Post-modern culture is defined by just such transgression and indeed by its indifference to it. In architecture and in literature, but most especially in the hybrid forms of the electronic media, through parody and pastiche, the world becomes real only in its reflections. But the mirrors are fun-fair mirrors. They reflect only to distort. When James Stirling leaves a block of Staatsgallerie marble lying on the pavement. When David Lynch or Quentin Tarantino construct their twisting, endlessly referential, narratives. When Madonna is Madonna, now and then, or not. On MTV or LiveTV. In all these and other places the media are playing, playing with each other and playing with us. And we in turn play with them. Their lack of seriousness is serious. Their seriousness is disarming. Their disarming is ironic. Their irony is compulsive, celebratory.

There are big questions to be asked here. Questions which require a deeper understanding of media as culture, and of the role of media in enabling or constraining individuality and freedom. Are we talking engagement or escape? Do we play to win or, in a late capitalist society, are we born to lose? What value lies in the game? What prizes are vouchsafed to the victors?

If you listen to the arch critics of the cultural industry, the answers are clear enough. The pleasures to be had from the games of mass culture deprive us of our critical judgement: 'To be pleased means to say Yes . . . Pleasure always means not to think about anything, to forget suffering even where it is shown. Basically it is helplessness. It is flight; not as is asserted flight from a wretched reality, but from the last remaining thought of resistance' (Horkheimer and Adorno, 1972: 144).

Perhaps, however, the game offers more (or less) than pleasure from time to time. Perhaps the play can, on occasion, be a rehearsal for the real: a practice. The flight simulator for the everyday. Maybe it can be a subversion. The parody debunks, punctures, undermines. Though it does not always work. Indeed play and pleasure are not the same thing. We play the wrong game, sometimes, and just as often we play badly. Yet there is something here, and something too in Horkheimer and Adorno's singling out of *chance* as a focus for the manipulative intent of the cultural industry. To value chance, to see it as the main principle of success, suggests that the prize can be won without effort and without responsibility. The lottery is the supreme metaphor of capitalism in this regard; the ultimate game, the power play.

Such judgements are tempting but perhaps too singular, too intolerant of contradiction and ambiguity. They are in any event suffused by an elitist asceticism which is common and persistent among the critics of mass culture. My games are OK; its yours that are bringing society to its knees.

I still want to preserve play, the play, the game. And even if I postpone judgement for the moment on its value, I still want to insist on its place in society and culture. I still want to think about the ways in which in play we can and do claim something of our individuality, constructing identities through the roles we take and the rules we follow. We are all players now in games, some or many of which the media make. They distract but they also provide a focus. They blur boundaries but still somehow preserve them. For, arguably we know, even as children, when we are playing and when we are not. The thresholds between the mundane and the heightened spaces of the everyday are still there to be crossed, and they are crossed each time we switch on the radio or the television, or log on to the World Wide Web. Playing is both escape and engagement. It occupies protected spaces and times on the screen, surrounding it and, at some further remove. While we can enter media spaces in other ways and for other purposes, for work or for information, for example, while they exist to persuade as well as to educate, the media are a principal site in and through which, in the securities and stimulation that they offer the viewers of the world, we play: subjunctively, freely, for pleasure.

And such play bridges not just inner and outer worlds and realities, but also the off-line and on-line worlds and realities. Let me end this chapter with a story told by my colleague Sonia Livingstone (1998: 436) from her recent research on new media and adolescent children. It goes as follows:

> Two eight year old boys play their favourite multimedia adventure game on the family PC. When they discover an Internet site where the same game could be played interactively with unknown others, this occasions great excitement in the household. The boys choose their fantasy personae, and try diverse strategies to play the game, both co-operative and competitive, simultaneously 'talking' on-line (i.e. writing) to the other participants. But

when restricted in their access to the Internet, for reasons of cost, the game spins off into 'real life'. Now the boys, together with their younger sisters, choose a character, dress up in battle dress, and play 'the game' all over the house, going downstairs to Hell, The Volcanoes and The Labyrinth, and upstairs to The Town, 'improving' the game in the process. This new game is called, confusingly for adult observers, 'playing the Internet'.

8 Performance

In 1958 a woman known as Agnes appeared at the Department of Psychiatry at UCLA. She saw a psychiatrist, Robert Stoller, and a sociologist, Harold Garfinkel. Born male, she was about to undergo surgery to enable a physiological transformation to the female she had in all visible respects already become and which she earnestly desired, completely, to be. Her case was reported intensively, but most especially by Garfinkel who saw in it a way of exploring, in turn, the ways in which social life was a matter for ongoing accomplishment. Using this exceptional case study, Garfinkel was able to show how a person such as Agnes has to learn, appropriate and manage, on a daily, hourly basis, a role into which she was not socialized, and in which failure would lead to unmasking and catastrophe. The task she had set herself was to secure and guarantee:

> the ascribed rights and obligations of an adult female by the acquisition and use of skills and capacities, the efficacious display of female appearances and performances, and the mobilizing of appropriate feelings and purposes. As in the normal case, the tests of such management work occurred under the gaze of and in the presence of normal male and female others. (Garfinkel, 1967: 134)

This is an activity which Garfinkel calls 'passing'. Passing is more than game-playing, though there are elements of the game within it. It is most significantly not a game because the boundaries which define the game space (and which enable any player to leave the field if necessary) are not there. Agnes's performance was necessarily continuous, and developmental. It was also a matter of life: a reality to be negotiated with her male lover, with herself, and with the society at large in its attention to and dependence upon the, albeit taken-for-granted, detail of daily interaction. Agnes wanted to be that taken-for-granted individual: the normal, ordinary, as she would see it, female. This is, Garfinkel argues, more than a matter of impression management (the castration signifies). He sees Agnes, *force majeure*, as an accomplished sociologist who, in the practical work of making herself into herself, understands deeply and personally that social life is indeed and thoroughly a matter of accomplishment:

'We learned from Agnes, who treated sexed persons as cultural events that members make happen, that members' practices alone produce the observable-tellable normal sexuality of persons, and do so only, entirely, exclusively in actual, singular, particular occasions through actual witnessed displays of common talk and conduct' (Garfinkel, 1967: 181). What does this 'case' tell us? What does it suggest for an enquiry into the role of media in social life and in experience?

It offers a particular version of the social and our place in, as well as our responsibility for, it. It presumes society to be a certain kind of thing. It presumes that social life depends not just on the play of objective circumstances, the conditions and conditioning of structure and history, but that it requires, in complex and subtle ways, our active participation. It also presumes that society cannot be made without us, and that the making of the social, its continuous reproduction, is enabled and performed through the minute-by-minute, and the *minute*, interactions that allow us to recognize and claim a certain normality, ordinariness, security and identity for ourselves and our fellows in the daily round.

There is a strong thread of this kind of reasoning in sociology and anthropology. Often, and correctly, criticized for its failures, precisely, to recognize the effects of history (that the world changes), power (that the circumstances under which we make our meanings are not often within our control), and irreconcilable difference (that social life is more than a matter of a negotiation and shared understandings, it is crucially full of conflict), such an approach nevertheless allows a considered focus on the dynamics of social life in such a way as to enable attention to the performative, to the ways in which society becomes art, and artifice becomes the social.

In such writing, and the work of Erving Goffman is pre-eminent, social life is seen as a matter of impression management. Our world is a world of visible appearance. We live in a presentational culture in which appearance *is* reality. Individuals and groups present their faces to the world in settings where they manage their performance with more or less confidence: front stages in which what we do we do for show, to impress others and define and maintain our sense of ourselves, a sense of identity; front stages which in turn depend on back stages where, out of sight of our intended audience, we can prepare the make-up, the make-over.

Such a perception of the social has a number of consequences and difficulties. It elides any ontological difference between truth and falsehood, since all presentations are to a degree misrepresentations. On the other hand, it reifies what might otherwise be seen as only a veneer of civility, granting substance to what could easily be seen as merely the superficial.

It also withdraws from moral judgement, and it insists that all society, not just our own, is the product of such performative action.

There are, however, a number of things that can be said and valued. The first is the perception that all action is communication. The second is that performance almost always involves idealization. The third is that the success of a performance, in everyday life as on the bounded spaces of stage and screen, depends on the judgements and acceptance of an audience. And the final point, and this is not Goffman's, but one made, critically, by others, is that modernity has brought with it, as it has encouraged and enabled the emergence of a more public private life, the intensification of such performative behaviours, behaviours which create both the social and the individual, and which allow the performer not just to present herself to the other but to reveal herself to herself – an essentially reflexive act.

Modernity has brought with it the personal appropriation of the ceremonial. Indeed, in this respect, as I shall presently suggest, the media have been crucial. It has also brought with it the opportunity to construct for ourselves a range of identities designed for different audiences in different settings. But modernity has also brought with it the possibility of *arguing* that even such a fundamental dimension of identity as gender can also be seen as performative. Judith Butler, for example, speaks of gender as a 'doing':

> words, acts, gestures, and desire produce the effect of an internal core or substance, but produce this *on the surface* of the body, through the play of signifying absences that suggest, but never reveal, the organising principle of identity as a cause. Such acts, gestures, enactments, generally construed, are *performative* in the sense that the essence or identity that they otherwise purport to express are *fabrications* manufactured and sustained through corporeal signs and other discursive means. That the gendered body is performative suggests that it has no ontological status apart from the various acts which constitute its reality. (Butler, 1990: 136, italics in original)

These performances are not just games. They are, like Agnes's, whom Butler seems not to know, in deadly earnest. Our lives and identities depend upon them. They become real, the real thing. In this view the social is a web of meaning which is sustainable as long as those meanings are held in common, as long as they are repeated, shared, communicated and, of course, imposed. Experience is constructed through these webs of meaning, the texts and discourses of the everyday, and experience in turn is dependent on our participation, enforced or otherwise, in the performative and in performance.

The terms that have been used in this discussion so far: accomplishment, presentation, performance, the performative, despite differences of emphasis and intent, all address the same issue, which should by now be clear. Together they provide a way of thinking about social life which privileges action, meaning and the power of the symbolic. Such a way of thinking about the social also offers an important route into thinking about the media and its significance.

The explanation for the role of the media in everyday life is, therefore, enabled precisely by the perception that the world in which we live, which we in part construct, and which is based on experience, our understanding of that experience and our attempt to represent (or misrepresent) it, is in one powerful, performative sense, already mediated. In this view, action itself is a kind of mediation. It already involves a problematization of the real and the distinction, if not the effacement of the distinction, between the material and the symbolic. It also involves a recognition that experience is more than behaviour, more than the passing of the moment, and that performance is both historically situated (always) and historically significant (sometimes), and that the things that we do, the roles we take, the games we play, the lives we lead, are the product of the complexities of culture in its widest sense: dependent on, but not necessarily determined by, the meanings, interests and influences of a social situation over which we have limited control.

Thus to see social life as having been performed, and to see such performance as a continuous, mostly but not always, taken-for-granted activity without which the shared and enabling symbolic realities of everyday life would crumble into dust, is to grant yet another dimension of the social as subjunctive. The transition from the taken-for-granted, daily rituals performed on buses, in banks and bars, to the exceptional public rituals of the high and mighty in real or virtual spaces, is a smooth, perhaps even an increasingly seamless, one. We know about performance, instinctively as it were, because we do it all the time. We know about performance, innocently as it were, because we see it in our media all the time. And even though we know about the boundaries between private and public spaces, as well as the differences between mediated and experienced realities, we know that the boundaries separate as well as connect: they are barriers as well as bridges. And, I would want to suggest, we move across them, and across the boundary between performer and audience, with increasing ease, as a matter of course.

Singing Cole Porter songs in the bath and dancing a solitary tango in the bedroom in private on the one hand; displaying a shareable identity through displays of fashion or in the act of voting, or participation in a public event, like the funeral of Diana, Princess of Wales, on the other. The media provide the wherewithal: the tools and the fantasies. Object lessons. Opportunities. The world is performed within our media on a daily basis. And we, its audience, perform alongside it, as players and as participants, mimicking and appropriating, and reflecting upon, its truths and its falsehoods. If we are to make the effort to understand the media then we need to make sense of this, its performative dimension: the encouragement and reinforcement of a culture of display, one which we appropriate into our everyday lives, and one which is continually sustained on screens and through speakers.

Consider the televising of Diana's funeral. And consider, if you will, the following.

I live in Central London. On the morning of the funeral I began to watch television as the cortège began its journey through Hyde Park, and then through familiar streets. Most striking perhaps was not the expected silent crowds nor the crunching hooves and crunching feet, but the rhythmic tolling of the Abbey bell, once every minute: a kind of passacaglia to the morning's events. Some time around 10.15, as the procession neared Whitehall, Jennifer and I decided to walk to the Abbey, not in the expectation of actually seeing anything, that is not in the expectation of actually seeing *her*, but more to take in the atmosphere, the silence, the emptiness of the city, the strangeness of it all and, of course, though perhaps more self-consciously, to participate in some way, to share, to claim, to own a piece of it.

We left the television on: the rest of the household was beginning to emerge. And we could hear the bell continuing to toll as we walked down the stairs to the front door and out into the sunshine. At the threshold we could still hear it, but now it came not from the television, it came from the Abbey. It was real. The same bell. The same sound. But real. We had in some simple but mysterious way punctured media space, moved from mediated reflection and representation into experience. In that moment we had, indeed seamlessly, mimicked the actions of the millions who left the safe, domestic unambiguousness of media representation and made the pilgrimage to London during those extraordinary days both before and during the funeral.

It is this passage, this escape from, this *appropriation of*, media space on which I want to reflect here, and to do so in the light of my discussion, in this chapter, of performance. The question is this: how and why is it that as the world media went into spasm on the death of Diana, Princess of Wales, millions upon millions of ordinary folk (and, of course, I was among them) decided to get up out of their armchairs, leave their front rooms, take the commuter train and *occupy* public space and, indeed, public time, since the public holiday that was the funeral was not declared, and the funeral itself, by all accounts, was created to fulfil the projections of those who wanted to be, needed to be, on the streets beside her.

Many explanations of such behaviour have already been offered. The key words have been mass hysteria, religious fervour, media manipulation. Each privileges a dimension of (mostly gendered) vulnerability, in which observed behaviour (and *pace* Max Weber, it is behaviour rather than motivated action that is being addressed) is defined, psychoanalytically, spiritually or sociologically, through a frame that gives little or no credibility to the capacity of individuals to take charge of, or responsibility for, what they feel, believe in or do. Of course, it is easy to be seduced into the opposite position, to romanticize our freedom from the collective forces of contemporary culture, to exaggerate the capacities of individuals to determine and to define for themselves their own positions in mass society. Both positions have truth within them. Both, on their own, are untenable. At issue of course, now, is how to understand the particularities, not the generalities, of these responses and the relationships they express and engender.

Arguably the key event in the fairy-tale that was her life, more Grimm than Andersen perhaps, was the BBC *Panorama* interview of 1995. In that television interview, and of course the consequent media response which electrifyingly fanned and intensified its content, Diana broke the bounds and, like those who subsequently occupied public space in her name, punctured the conventions of the media's representation of royalty.

These conventions, and they have been well analysed by David Chaney (1983), involve the emergence of an increasing tension between public and private, symbol and reality. The construction of the royal family as media figures, to become the symbolic centres of Britain's forlorn attempt at nation-building during the twentieth century, involved a delicate manoeuvre to preserve their status while at the same time making them accessible and human. The parallels with the Hollywood star system have, of course, been noted and they are intensely relevant, as Elton John's choice of musical epitaph made crystal clear. While it is certain that television was a key medium in this project, and the 1953 Coronation the beginning, it was the marriage itself which involved a major shift of gear, a shift of course, in which wittingly or unwittingly the Palace colluded.

The *Panorama* interview created a new space, a space that was outside the media frame, though of course essentially still contained by it. The balance between symbol and reality had, possibly permanently, been shifted; not because she attacked the Palace (though that was hardly likely to be inconsequential) but because she displayed more humanity than she was allowed. Of course, all of this was premeditated, much of it was coached, and some of it was, probably, disingenuous. Yet the desire to be a 'Queen of Hearts' (as much as the achievement of becoming the 'People's Princess') severed the head, and enabled her to occupy – though still as symbol – a transcendent space. The hagiography began at that point. What was signified above all was the possibility of breaking the bounds. It was a lesson that was to be vividly learned, and which was reproduced by the million in the actions of those who subsequently broke their own media bounds and, though still contained and indeed increasingly exploited by the media, occupied the streets of London.

We are told that, in the media age, there is no escape from the simulacra. That everything we touch is mediated, transformed, poisoned by media. That the boundaries between reality and fantasy, truth and falsehood, fact and fiction can no longer be determined, are no longer any use. This is indeed what we are told. But such a position downgrades experience to insignificance. It is empirically vacuous. It is frighteningly amoral. Even if it is easy to exaggerate the power of the popular demonstration (which was far from being a popular revolt) and to intimate, as the press were not slow to do, that this might signal the end of the monarchy, indeed the end of life in Britain as we know it; and, even if the Republic is not yet at hand, it would be a terrible mistake to consign the actions and feelings of so many to the dustbin of mediation.

To walk among those who gathered before and during the funeral was to walk among (and this is not romance) ordinary people: families, generations, ethnically diverse, middle, mostly suburban, England, who were not just taking the media air, but actively participating in an event which without them would be meaningless. There was tourism and voyeurism of course (and I, in part, was both tourist and voyeur), but there was also a powerful set of claims and connections: women identifying with the woman, children identifying with the child, parents identifying with the parent, lovers with the lovers, dreamers with the shattered dreams. And these identifications, these connections, were acted upon. They were performed. The ritual was being invented in real time. And public space was being occupied. You could smell the lilies.

No matter that this whole performance was in turn appropriated, not to say encouraged and sustained, by the media themselves. The performance itself was a popular appropriation in which meanings were shared and in which shared experiences were forged and would be remembered. And performance, indeed, is what it was, a 'doing and a thing done, drifting between past and present, presence and absence, consciousness and memory' (Diamond, 1996: 5). In this performance, performed for the self and performed for the other, participants claimed ownership of an event which in those very claims clawed it back from the clutches of the media. In this performance, daily played out both in front of, and beyond the reach of, television cameras and the notebooks of journalists, we put our own stamp on things.

Performing Diana. We did it. Huge numbers of us. The nation. Its people. With and without, alongside and against, the media. Occupying public space, filling private space; blurring boundaries; reflecting mirrors. Integrating the personal experience with the collective, and distilling both through the image of a life performed. Once again the exceptional provides illumination for the ordinary: our infinite capacity to participate in the collective, and in so doing to create it in the shared and endlessly mediated dramas of everyday life. In this process, and in these performances, the media signify, though not always in a straightforward or obvious fashion. Indeed, the border between mediated experience and that supposedly unmediated is impossible to draw. Studying the media requires attention to this and the exploration of its consequences.

Yet perhaps this is not the whole story. Perhaps this performative effervescence can be seen in other ways, and read against this visible grain. Is there not something else happening here, something perhaps more complex, and maybe even disturbing?

If we are to suppose that modernity has produced what might be described, and Jurgen Habermas (1989) does so describe it, as the refeudalization of the public sphere; if we are to accept, at least in part, Guy Debord's trenchant (1977) critique of what he calls the society of the spectacle, both of whom see in the appropriation of performative culture by the combined dark forces of capitalism and the state a constriction of freedom and imagination; if indeed we acknowledge that public culture has been privatized through the attention of the media, and *per contra* that private culture has been publicized, then we have, for better or worse, to recognize a profound change in the location and character of performance in everyday life.

The Diana funeral provides, in an exaggerated but triumphant way, an example of the way in which the blurring of audience and performer takes place on a public stage, both in the media and beyond its reach (though, of course, never completely beyond its reach). It also takes place on a stage, as a result of its mediation, which removes it from the realm of the personal and transforms each moment into a fragment of a national or even a global event.

We might want, as a consequence, to think about it quite differently. To think of our participation in the funeral not as a shared and committing moment, but as a performance without responsibility; a sharing of private grief without public mourning. A ritual that is out of time: the last gasp of a communion without a god or indeed, *pace* Durkheim, without society. Indeed the effervescence disperses in the gradual trickling away of Diana's image on the covers of the tabloids and the weeklies as the days and weeks pass by. A year later the British media failed almost completely to reproduce the passion or the engagement of that initial moment. A year later there was little left, and little, crucially, to reproduce. Only vague shapes, vague shadows. The shared meanings of the moment, genuinely felt and dramatically enshrined in public action, could be seen to be part of an experience that, at best, could only return to the private and to the personal. What the media give, they also take away.

The audience for the funeral was an anonymous one; and since we did not know it, or them, since we did not know our fellow players, it lost much of its significance. Our own performance could be said to refract only the self: solipsistically, narcissistically. What passed for the social was created on a public stage among strangers. The social was left to our imagination, and to the memory of an event in which we both did and did not participate.

What is missing in such engagements is the shudder of connection, of attention, of command. Entry into media space in the search for the social is fraught and vulnerable.

Consider the Home Page. Randomly I type a name. Donna Chung. I arrive at a site called Friends' Homepages. It lists 38 names, one of which is indeed Donna Chung. Most of those listed are students at Yale, but not all. Donna Chung has her picture, her address and her telephone number and a link to a cell group. Christopher Pan, a philosophy major, class of '98, is a name further down the list. His page reads as follows:

> Wow . . . my very own slice of 'cyber-' real estate. Great.
> 'Nothing much to say, i guess, just the same as all the rest . . .'
> I appreciate your visit, and hope that you bear with me as I continue to figure out how all this stuff works. I would appreciate it even more if you let me know that you indeed did visit, so that I can take comfort in the realization that people DO actually look at this stuff. I've got some grand plans for this little bit of of realty. We'll see how it turns out.
>
> Some basic facts about me, as I stall for interesting things to say:
>
> Christopher Pan
> born: November 4, 1976 in New Haven, CT
> Yale University
> Davenport College
> Class of 1998
> Philosophy major
> e-mail: christopher.pan@yale.edu
> real mail: p.o. box 201704, New Haven, CT 06520
> telephone: (203) 436 0291

There are links to a series of pictures of himself and his family, including one of his sister at Stanford with an invitation to e-mail her too.

What's going on here? What kind of performance is this? Here is a body in cyberspace, floating like a grain of dust in the electronic ether. A personal display, a call for attention (his plea for a response signifies), a singular, private stage; a solitary performance in virtual space. There is no audience here. No guarantee of attention. Here too performance carries no responsibility and no engagement. The randomness of the communication matches the randomness of the crowd at a public event. Yet a society of a sort forms within these communications: the electronic links construct an invisible and momentarily significant network of connections: to other folk, to other places, to other sites. I can follow them without any disturbance. I can create them without any damage. I can tell the world who I am, or who I would like to be (and follow this up on chat-lines and Usenet Groups), and I will not be called to account. My accomplishment is defined by my capacity and competence to create an image. But there is creativity here, and energy, as well as playfulness. Technology has given me a stage. I can perform on it. I can claim a space. If someone would only listen.

We have come a long way from Agnes in which performance was a matter of social life or death. We have even moved beyond Diana, in which the final performance of a public persona inspired a spontaneous multi-mediated ritual of shared communion. The more thoroughly our identities come to depend on the play of electronic media, the more deeply embedded our media come to be in experience, and the more a virtual society (if such a thing exists) encourages and enables performance without audience and performativity without consequence, then, it might be suggested, the more we may find ourselves alone. Is this not something we need to understand better than we do now?

9 Consumption

I am arguing that we must study the media because the media are central to experience. They inform, reflect, express experience, our experience, on a daily basis. I have suggested that such study must involve thinking about media not as a series of institutions or products or technologies, or not only these things, but that it must involve thinking about media as a process, as a process of mediation. Media is done. We do it. And it is done to us. So far I have discussed some of these ideas through an analysis of the ways in which media are involved in play and performance. Both are key activities in which as social beings we engage with the world around us, and in so doing contribute to it and define our place within, or our claims upon, it.

In this chapter I want to add another dimension of experience. One which overlaps, inevitably, with both play and performance, and indeed in which, it could be suggested, both play and performance are mobilized in the service of our participation in economic life. In this chapter I want to discuss consumption and media's relationship to it. Pay, play and display.

Consumption is a contrary and a sometime thing. It is an activity, individual and collective, private and public, that depends on the destruction of goods for the production of meanings. It mediates between thrift and excess, economy and extravagance. It allays anxieties about our capacity to survive and prosper with respect to both subsistence and status, and yet it succeeds in stemming, once and for all, neither anxiety, need nor desire. On the contrary. Retail therapy is both the cure and the disease.

Consumption operates between work and leisure. Indeed, it is work *and* leisure, undertaken in the spaces and times released by the tyrannical rhythms of industrial society, yet pursued with a relentless and dogged enthusiasm which blurs the boundaries between the indentured and the free so beloved of ascetic Protestantism and of capitalism, both.

Sunday trading. Consumption is hard work. It is the work of production, work undertaken by global consumer-citizens as individuals construct both personal meanings and claims to participate in local cultures. It is work that links individuals and collectivities together, defined by, defining and sharing taste, status or need. From the homogenizing outputs of Levi-Strauss, Kangol and Sony are derived the particularities of style; the moments of fashion and identity crafted by groups, young or ethnically distinct, whose power in the formal economy and hence whose full participation in global society is limited or, except in these moments of marginal creativity, pretty non-existent. Consumption is a way of mediating and moderating the horrors of standardization. And shopping is just the beginning. A stage in the life-cycle of the commodity, but one which has neither beginning nor end: a continuous, constant play of products and meanings, iteratively, dialectically shifting attention away from the pain of extraction or manufacture and towards the object, its image and its appropriation in use.

Focus groups and market research create the new geography of consumption, a geography of global distribution networks and an infinity of consumption decisions; a geography which links the corner shop to the global distribution network; a geography of malls and department stores, of teleshopping and electronic commerce; a geography in which time is confined to the micro-moves of the product cycle and managed obsolescence; a time–space geography limited to the minutiae of market shares and customer satisfaction; to the matching of image and identity; and to the just-in-time production and distribution of the latest fashion garment which links local needs to global satisfaction and, of course, vice versa.

To buy, or not to buy. That is the question.

As Arjun Appadurai (1996: 83) suggests:

> We are all housekeepers now, labouring daily to practice the disciplines of purchase in a landscape whose temporal structures have become radically polyrhythmic. Learning these multiple rhythms (of bodies, products, fashions, interest rates, gifts and style) and how to integrate them is not just work – it is the hardest sort of work, the work of the imagination.

The point, of course, that is being made here is that consumption is the one single core activity through which we engage on a daily basis, in the culture of our times. Consumption is an activity that is not at all bounded with the decision or act of purchase, nor is it singular. We consume continuously and through our capacity to do so we contribute to, reproduce and in no small measure affect the texture of experience. In this we are aided by the media. Indeed consumption and mediation in numerous respects are fundamentally interdependent. We consume media. We consume through the media. We learn how and what to consume through the media. We are persuaded to consume through the media. The media, it is not too far fetched to suggest, consume us. And, as I have already suggested, and will continue to argue, consumption is itself a form of mediation, as the given values and meanings of objects and services are translated and transformed into the languages of the private, the personal and the particular. We consume objects. We consume goods. We consume information. We consume images. But in that consumption, in its daily taken-for-grantedness, we make our own meanings, negotiate our own values, and in so doing we make our world meaningful. I am what I buy; no longer what I make or, indeed, think. And so, I expect, are you.

Most of consumption is, therefore, quite taken for granted. Big decisions are agonized over, maybe. But millions of small ones are entirely matter of fact. So much so that consumption has either been ignored completely, at least until recently, in the literature, or on those occasions when it is has been discussed it is condemned as either peripheral to the real business of life or immoral. It is seen as female work and therefore denied significance. It is noticed only in excess. Only when it is conspicuous. Yet consumption makes the world go round. And, arguably, increasingly and insistently so: 'Consumption is an active mode of relations (not only to objects, but to the collectivity and to the world), a systematic mode of activity and a global response on which our whole cultural system is founded' (Baudrillard, 1988: 21).

Baudrillard is not wrong. Increasingly our individual status in society is no longer defined by our position in the relations of production, as the boundaries between classes wither on the vine of the decline of manufacturing and the commensurate rise of service industries and the white collar. Our identities are claimed, instead, through the subtle, and sometimes not so subtle, positioning of display. The map of difference, the one which enables us to chart our way through the hierarchies of wealth and power, is defined by our capacity to position ourselves and to read the marks of consumption. The flat cap is no longer an indicator of class, but of status, and indeed an indicator and a status that will change with the seasons.

These claims, and our capacity to make and sustain them, are of course one of the abiding rhetorics of everyday life. Consumption involves an acting out. The play of fantasy. The display of identity. We are offered commodities by a capitalist system almost perennially in a crisis of overproduction. We are being asked to see customers as the kings and queens of the market-place, but this is a delusion that expresses the anxieties of a system unable to claim the necessary control over consumption decisions rather than the realities of economic power. Yet the tension is there. Fantasies must be offered and embodied in the images of the advertisement, in the manipulations of the market-place. Yet they cannot be fulfilled. And they must not be fulfilled. On the contrary. They must be sustained, eternally. The commodities that we are offered are the product of an alienating system of production on which we entirely depend, yet at the same time they offer us the raw materials for creating our own sense of ourselves. Such is its paradox. As Appadurai (1996: 82) remarks, 'The fact is that consumption is now the social practice through which persons are drawn into the work of fantasy. It is the daily practice through which nostalgia and fantasy are drawn together in a world of commodifed objects.'

In a fascinating and suggestive essay Arjun Appadurai discusses the culture of consumption as central to modernity, but not unique to it. What links our own consumption practices with those of our forebears lies in consumption's relationship to time. I want to follow his argument here a little further because it provides a powerful entry into a set of questions about the media's role in consumption, and it also allows me to explore an aspect of experience so far under-played: its temporality.

He starts with an observation that consumption is, of its essence, repetitive. Bodily needs require continuous attention. The body as a socially and historically specific thing, the focus of concern, discipline, display. Such consumption becomes, is required to be, a habit. And habit in turn requires regulation. Societies have created mechanisms, proper locations and proper rhythms, for the regulation of consumption. The days are marked by the appropriate places and times for eating. The seasons are marked by our willingness to consume and celebrate whatever ripens. The calendar is marked by events and rituals which highlight the process of consumption, marking the year by the drama of planting or of harvest, denying or indulging, both fast and feast. And such markers are still very much with us. Appadurai suggests, however, that when it comes to consumption the natural does not define the cultural and the temporal. Rather the reverse, for in his view it is consumption which organizes life, and the rituals, both large and small, that we construct around consumption actually create time rather than merely reflect it. Christmas is a case in point, especially if we consider the complex patterns of time that are associated with its preparation and management. It all comes down, of course, to shopping, and to how best and when to do it (ideally in plenty of time, even more ideally, from an economic perspective, in the post-Christmas sales). Christmas from this perspective is not simply a seasonal fact but a year-long celebration (Appadurai, 1996: 70).

Societies have gone through what we have called retrospectively the 'consumer revolution' in different ways. The move from interdiction to fashion via sumptuary regulation, which Norbert Elias (1978) detected as the interface between consumption and civilization, is a general one, but it has emerged as a result of different forces and had different consequences, depending on the where and the how of it. Consumption has had a different history in the United States, in Europe and in India, and that history itself is a product both of general social changes and the particular dynamics of taste, social power and the emergence of the market which have affected individual societies and groups in distinctive ways.

The objects that we now value and purchase embody a complex and contradictory kind of temporality mediating, as they do, authenticity, patina and novelty. The past elides with the future, nostalgia with desire. Our advertising teaches us to miss things we have never lost and mass consumption is an exercise in time management: regulating fantasy and structuring the ephemeral. And fashion is its most profound expression:

> As far as the experience of time is concerned, the pleasure that lies at the centre of modern consumption is neither the pleasure of the tension between fantasy and utility nor the tension between individual desire and collective disciplines. . . . [The] pleasure that has been inculcated into the subjects who act as modern consumers is to be found in the tension between nostalgia and fantasy, where the present is represented as if it were already past. This inculcation of the pleasure of ephemerality is at the heart of the disciplining of the modern consumer. . . . [It] expresses itself at a variety of social and cultural levels: the short shelf life of products and lifestyles; the speed of fashion change; the velocity of expenditure; the polyrhythms of credit, acquisition and gift; the transience of television-product images; the aura of periodization that hangs over both products and lifestyles in the imagery of the mass media. (Appadurai, 1996: 83–4)

From these arguments Appadurai constructs the outline of an aesthetics of ephemerality. It is, he suggests, the ground base of civilization in its contemporary form, mediating and moderating the effects of a global culture and the consequences of a global economic regime flattered by a presumption of rationality and consistency. 'Modern consumption seeks to replace the aesthetics of duration with the aesthetics of ephemerality' (Appadurai, 1996: 85). Well, yes and no.

There is something missing in this powerful mix of wanting, remembering, being and buying. It is a sense of the rhythmic and the cyclical. And it is a sense of time as a structure. To fix on the ephemeral is to buy into the ideology of the mass market and not to see that the ephemeral is itself dependent on the continuities, the predictabilities, the rhythms of the calendar. We only desire and manage the ephemeral because we know it is permanent. We are only happy with the spontaneous and the new because we are confident in the consistencies of the continuous. And in this the media keep us going.

Much has been written about the quality of time in a globalizing and post-modern society. It no longer features as a constraint. It has no limits. It is compressed. The forces of commodification, the demands of capitalism in a world economy that seems to have to go faster in order just to stay still, the particular character of information as a global, weightless, transparent product and resource, have changed time irrevocably. It has been removed from experience, from the metronomic, the regularities of the clock, from the human, from the body, from the seasons. Work now is continuous. Production is too. The digital watch marks time as a continuous process, where time consists of a series of points: eight fifty-four, eight fifty-five, eight fifty-six. It no longer marks time, as the sweeping hands of the analogue watch have done, as a set of relationships and positions: five *to* nine, a quarter *past* eight, noon. Time no longer needs to be read.

Commodified time, the time which regulates consumption is, in these arguments therefore, both continuous and ephemeral. The two are crucially interrelated. The media are the instruments to persuade us to increase the level and intensity of our consumption activities. The home-shopping TV channels, the web-sites which offer electronic trading, are no slaves to the timetable or to natural rhythms. They are boundless, eternal. Time is reduced to insignificance, an individual matter. Time, consumption, mediation together become desocialized, dependent on nothing other than the eccentricity of the moment.

This certainly seems to be the trend, at least as it is read from the vantage points of metropolitan cultures. It is not yet, however, the whole story. Everyday life is still, for most of us, a complex of different times and temporal pressures. Marked still by the sequencing of work and leisure, or weekdays and weekends which, despite their erosion, require us to synchronize activities with each other. Marked too by the requirements to participate in routines that, notwithstanding their origins in a mechanical age, still provide comfort as well as control. Unbounded consumptive time is not yet nor uniformly transcendent. A daily life is still a daily life. And its rhythms are still dependent on our participation in the cultures of consumption and mediation. Time is still a finite resource. So what will become of time in an age of infinite consumption and eternal mediation? Another question which goes to the heart of things.

Paddy Scannell (1988) has documented how the media have become central to our perception and organization of time: how they provide an order within the calendar through the regularities of national and global events; how they mark, in a similar fashion, the rhythms of the week and the day through the consistencies of schedules, themselves designed somehow to replicate as well as reinforce the supposed rhythms of daily life. Yet here, as elsewhere, time is the site of struggle. The temporality of the media is a crucial dimension of their rhetorical apparatus; calling us, claiming us to accept their definitions of appropriateness. Calling us to stop, perhaps, what we are doing, to attend, to participate in shared time, to be one among the millions watching prime-time news or a popular soap opera. And calling us to attend, too, to the media as objects of consumption, as well as facilitators of consumption.

As I have suggested, we buy the media, we buy through the media and we buy as a result of what we see and hear on the media. The rhythms of the broadcast, of the sponsored programming of the narrowcast, of the pulsing banners on the Internet, together, are also the rhythms of consumption. The great mediated events of the year require our participation as consumers, exchanging gifts, buying souvenirs. The minor moments of radio or television or web encourage us likewise: a punctuated continuity of advertising and sponsorship; gobbets of commerce in less than innocent texts. In television advertising time–space compression has another meaning: the technical squeezing of thirty-six seconds of content into a thirty-second slot (Jhally, 1990: 81).

Consumption has been, perhaps it still is, and necessarily, a social activity. We are not only concerned with our capacity to display the products of our skill as competent consumers, but we also appear to be concerned with the process of consumption as something we wish to share, and which provides a moment of sociability in an otherwise lonely life. Twenty-four hour shopping, like twenty-four hour news, is a resource to be managed and one that many of us will not need – though need is an uncomfortable concept in this context. Yet it provides, obviously enough, flexibility. It signals the beginning of the submergence of patterned and differentiated time, like the sea smoothing a wrinkled beach. Another consequence, perhaps, of global warming.

Indeed the market for advertising on the Internet is expected to reach billions in the next few years. Electronic commerce, a rising proportion of which will be individual acts of consumption, is growing rapidly too. These new media, above all the Internet, do indeed invite us to continuous consumption. Acts of homage to mammon unconstrained by ritual, undifferentiated by calendar, untouched by human hand. Yet early research suggests that electronic commerce is hindered by a lack of trust in the undifferentiated virtual spaces of the Internet: spaces where transactions take place God knows where, both dislocated and vulnerable to trespass.

Trust is important and I'll return to it.

In the meantime, there is *my* time to consider. So many of the arguments, and mine too thus far, presume in some sense an infinity of time both at the point of consumption and in the control of the consumer. Globalizing time, compressed time, homogeneous, ephemeral, continuous time, all make no obeisance to time as a scarce resource. When the sociologist Pierre Bourdieu focused his attention on the French as a nation of consumers, and used his study to explore how consumption enabled the minute, but class-specific, differentiations of taste and status that in turn resulted in the social geomorphology of the country, he pretty much forgot to consider both time and the media. The result, despite its originality and rigorous attention to detail, was a static and wooden analysis, which had little to say about consumption as a process that was itself historically as well as sociologically specific. The French could be distinguished by the ownership of both economic and cultural capital: they were rich, or poor, in material resources as well as symbolic resources, and the two were not coincident. The *nouveaux riches* had money but no class. The artist, or the academic, had class (at least in France) but no money. But how much time did they have, and how did they use what time they had to do what?

In the late twentieth century consumption is neither indentured nor free. Time has to be allocated for it, and not all of us either have enough of it nor manage it very well. We can therefore be distinguished, and significantly so, according not just to the amount of economic or cultural capital we can mobilize but also with respect to the amount of temporal capital. Temporal capital is gendered. Middle-class, home-based, child-rearing women have very little. Their husbands rather more. The unemployed are flush with it. However, temporal capital is not just a matter of quantity, but also quality. And our capacity to use what we have, and use it well, is of course dependent on our command of both material and symbolic resources. Time is precious and scarce for many. Empty and useless for many more. Such differentiation makes nonsense of the arguments about time as being uniform. It also makes time much more interesting and the media's role in its definition, allocation and consumption more complex. For in consumption we consume time. And in time we consume and are consumed.

The media mediate between time and consumption. They provide frameworks and exhortations. They are themselves consumed in time. Fashions are created and annulled. Novelty proclaimed and denied. Purchases made and declined. Ads watched and ignored. Rhythms sustained and rejected. Consumption. Convenience. Extravagance. Thrift. Identity. Display. Fantasy. Longing. Desire. All reflected and refracted on the screens, the pages and the sounds of our media. The culture of our times.

Locations of action and experience

In this section the focus shifts. It shifts towards the geography of the media, and it shifts towards questions that once again address the media as mediator. The concern is with context and consequence. We engage with media as social beings in different ways and from different places. The frameworks from within which we watch and listen, muse and remember, are defined in part by where we are in the world, and where we think we are, and sometimes too, of course, by where we might wish to be.

The spaces of media engagement, the spaces of media experience, are both real and symbolic. They are dependent on location, and on the routines that define our positions in time and space. The routines that mark the realities of movement and stasis in our everyday lives. The routines that define the sites of and for media consumption. Sitting in front of the screen or beside the keyboard. In personal, private, but also, as we have already seen, in public space. It is not just the movie which is on location.

How do these spatial co-ordinates affect media experience? How does media experience affect our perceptions of ourselves in the world? How can we begin to understand space and location as both objective: a sitting room, an address, temporary, permanent; and as subjective, a product of longing or dreaming? And how do the media engage with us in both these dimensions? Can they fix us in social and physical space? Does it matter where we watch and listen? What kind of space or spaces do the media offer or deny us?

These questions are important precisely because space has become a much more complex entity than perhaps we imagined it once to be. Modernity has brought with it both geographical and social mobility, an uprooting which successive industrial and political stimuli have reinforced, both in constructive and destructive ways. Many of us, increasing numbers of us, can no longer depend on the securities and stabilities of place. Can the media compensate for that loss? Do they reinforce it?

Knowing where we are is as important as knowing who we are, and of course the two are intimately connected; but the where and the who of it are complicated not just by the objective circumstances of location and the limits that they impose on our ability to act in and on the world, but by the media's capacity to extend reach and range: to offer a window on the world that increasingly is not just a window, but an invitation to extend our own capacity to act beyond the constraints of the immediate and the physical. Indeed into virtual space.

I want, then, in what follows, to explore these questions by fixing on three interweaving dimensions, or levels even, of action and mediation: home, community, globe. Each offers an opportunity not just to consider the objective characteristics of life and communication in social and media space: to enquire into the politics and culture of the household, or the neighbourhood or the global system. But it also offers an opportunity to explore each as an *imaginary*: as a site whose meaning and significance are constructed as part of culture in the dreams and narratives of media and everyday life. This is, or so it seems to me, where we must investigate the media's role, defining and articulating space and place, securing and disturbing us, both holding and withholding identity, placing us at the centre or the margins, and offering us the resources to transcend the limits of our immediate social space. Home, community and globe, in both their seamless and contradictory interrelationship, will enable me, too, to enquire into the media's role in enabling or disabling a sense of belonging.

10 House and home

A little girl, no more than five or six, comes home from school on a summer's afternoon. She runs into the sitting room of her suburban house, throws her empty lunch box on the sofa, and switches on the television. She plonks herself in front of it, kneeling on the rug. After a few minutes the garden beckons and out she goes. Down to the bottom and the swing. The television set is still on, and mother, from her panoptic view in the kitchen, noticing that her daughter is no longer watching, comes in and switches it off. The girl reacts immediately and as soon as her mother has left the sitting room runs back in, switches it on, and returns to the swing, barely in earshot.

What can be made of this fragment of everyday life? What might it tell us about the media's role? What questions does it suggest?

This is the childhood world of house and home. A garden. A kitchen. A mother. Safe. Secure. And within it, now, media. The television. On or off. On *and* off. Always available. Always to hand. Embedded in the culture of the household. A source of discord but also of dependence. Its familiarity, its continuity, its eternity.

There is much to be said about house and home and about our media's role in defining, enabling, as well as undermining it. And it is these contrary and contradictory dimensions of experience and their location, their grounding in the physical and psychical space of our own domesticity, that I want to consider now. For we can no longer think about home, any longer than we can live at home, without our media.

Home is an intensely evocative concept, especially, perhaps, in the twentieth century, a century in which it might be seen to have become most vulnerable. Indeed, such concepts, pregnant with nostalgia, emerge at their most insistent at times when it is recognized that, perhaps, they are no longer secure in the real world. The same fate has befallen family, community, or even society. They are suddenly recovered in the discourses of both the academy and daily life as they are about to disappear as effective social structures or institutions. Indeed whole disciplines, most especially that of sociology, have emerged like phoenixes from the ashes of this supposedly dying world. Whole political ideologies, more recently, have a similar source.

The English language is suffused with phrases about home that both depend on, and evoke, powerful emotions: to feel at home, homecoming, homelessness. Home sweet home. Home, in romance and desire, as a place for everything, where everything is in its place. And the media, too, in their soap operas and situation comedies, both directly and indirectly, provide equally powerful and insistent representations of what it is to be at home, as well as presuming, at least during the age of broadcasting, that they have a role in sustaining house and home. So such a discussion must go to the heart of things: indeed, to the hearth of things.

Therefore, to talk of home and hearth is at once not just to talk of a single physical space. It is to talk of a space which has a profound psychic charge. One in which memory colludes with and often contradicts desire. A place rather than a space. A place of shelter. A facilitating as well as an oppressive place. A place with boundaries to define and defend. A place of return. A place from which to view the world. Private. Personal. Inside. Familiar. Mine. All these terms have their opposite. And home is the product of their distinction. It is always relative. Always set against the public, the impersonal, the outside, the unfamiliar, yours. Home, as opposed to household or family, each describing different kinds of domesticity, seems to have had an unequivocal life; never once offering anything less than hope, a measure of longing.

The French philosopher Gaston Bachelard, in his remarkable book on the poetics of space, writes of home as the site of the to-ing and fro-ing of outside and inside. We might think of this as a dialectic of public and private, but also of the conscious and the unconscious. Home is, for him, in this sense a product of that dialectic as well as, in the context of everyday life, its precondition. I want to suggest that the media are involved, centrally, in this dialectic of inside and outside.

Let me follow Bachelard in his critical musings for a moment:

> We should therefore have to say how we inhabit our vital space, in accord with all the dialectics of life, how we take root, day after day, in a 'corner of the world'.
>
> For our house is our corner of the world. As has often been said, it is our first universe, a real cosmos in every sense of the word. If we look at it intimately, the humblest dwelling has beauty . . . all really inhabited space bears the essence of the notion of home. . . . A house constitutes a body of images that give mankind proofs or illusions of stability. We are constantly re-imagining its reality: to distinguish all these images would be to describe the soul of the house; it would mean developing a veritable psychology of the house. (Bachelard, 1964: 4, 17)

Bachelard's concern, a phenomenological concern, is with the status of house as home. It is one which, as he says, provides both the realities and metaphors for our security in an endlessly troubled world. We never leave our first house. The house from within which we construct our own universe, our own cosmic space. But the house also furnishes mirrors and models of the mind. The cellar is the unconscious, dark and damp in its subterranean forces: primitive and clammy. The attic is the source of cerebral fears, more easily rationalized but none the less monstrous for all that. As he suggests: 'a house that has been experienced is not an inert box. Inhabited space transcends geometrical space' (Bachelard, 1964: 47).

And inhabited space has doors, and thresholds:

> How concrete everything becomes in the world of the spirit when an object, a mere door, can give images of hesitation, temptation, desire, security, welcome and respect. If one were to give an account of all the doors one has closed and opened, of all the doors one would like to re-open, one would have to tell the story of one's entire life. (Bachelard, 1964: 224)

Homes and houses involve comings and goings, moves from inside to outside and the reverse. Thresholds to cross. Doors to open. Walls to defend. The boundaries between different kinds of spaces, and the values accorded to each, vary from culture to culture and from time to time. The city feels differently about its doors than the suburb. The Italian from the English. The middle from the working class. The polished step, the lace curtains, the verandas and the picture windows, all signal and signify a different version of the barrier between inside and out: to see and not be seen, to be seen and not to see. To welcome or to hide. To move freely or feel constrained. Front stages and back stages. Solitary and shared. Openings and closings. 'But is he who opens the door and he who closes it the same being?' (Bachelard, 1964: 224).

The door and its lintel mark the threshold. The threshold in turn is marked as sacred. Traditionally, Jewish households place a small casket, a mezzuzah, on the right door-post. As it is crossed it is touched and a prayer is said: 'may God keep my going out and my coming in from now on for ever more . . .'. The anthropologist, Arnold van Gennep, suggests that this crossing and the different kinds of spaces that are defined as a result, is a model for all ritual and for the ways in which societies have felt the need to distinguish between the sacred and secular, the ordinary and the highly charged; and to see and frame those differences spatially. The door has then both literal and spiritual significance. We dream of doors. Our shared and shareable fantasies are told as passages through doors: doors of perception, doors on the other side of which we will discover mysteries, pleasures and terrible nightmares. Alice through the looking glass.

Van Gennep (1960: 12, 20) is quite clear:

> Sacredness is an attribute not an absolute; it is brought into play by the nature of particular situations . . . the door is the boundary between the foreign and the domestic worlds in the case of an ordinary dwelling, between the profane and the sacred worlds in the case of a temple. Therefore to cross the threshold is to unite oneself with a new world.

And the one who controls the entries and the exits controls much of what is important both to media and to everyday life.

And now we have new doors, marked by the threshold of the television or computer screen. Doors and windows which allow us to see and to reach beyond the limits of the physical space of the house, beyond, indeed, imagination. To switch on, to log on, is to transcend physical space, of course. But it is to enter, as it always has been, even in a world of print, a marked territory, one which offers a glimpse of something sacred; ordinary but other worldly; powerful in its capacity to give us the illusion, and on occasion the reality, of control gained and exercised; powerful, too, in what it is often believed to be capable of doing to us. Indeed, where in the world is personal power other than double-edged? To reach is also to be reached. Our struggles over the media, both the private ones and the public ones, are struggles over this threshold.

In the UK public broadcasters accept the constraints of what is known, percipiently, as *the* threshold, the bewitching hour, 9 pm, at which children are perceived no longer to be watching and the broadcasters are released from some of the constraints on propriety. Time too has its doors. The anxieties that have fed and funded media research from its very beginning, starting perhaps with the Payne Fund studies on film in the 1930s, but entirely intensified in the age of television, are based on this fear of unwelcome things crossing a threshold. And, more recently, with telephone chat lines, bulletin boards, and pornographic or politically unacceptable global networks, these anxieties have become even more visible. We now fear that we can no longer control any threshold: neither that of the nation nor that of the home. The fear of penetration and of pollution is intense. The rites and rights of passage. I will return to this theme.

Our concern with security and with home is inevitably accompanied by concerns to protect it. The mother in my opening illustration may have been more keen to switch off the television to save electricity than to shut out an otherwise necessary evil. But for the daughter the machine was part of home. Its familiarity, and maybe even the distant sounds of signature tunes of favourite programmes, sufficed to provide her with comfort, electronically distributed, but none the less real, for her, for all that.

As Agnes Heller (1984: 239) indicates, home is the base for our actions and our perceptions, wherever we are:

> Integral to the average everyday life is awareness of a fixed point in space, a firm position from which we 'proceed' . . . and to which we return in due course. This firm position is what we call 'home'. . . . 'Going home' should mean: returning to that firm position which we know, to which we are accustomed, where we feel safe, and where our emotional relationships are at their most intense.

And when we cannot go home? And when we are on the move, displaced by wars, politics or the desire for a better life? We can, with our media, take something of home with us: the newspaper, the video, the satellite dish, the Internet. In this sense, and it has become a familiar trope of much recent theorizing on the new information age, home has become, and can be sustained as, something virtual, as without location. A place without space, to compensate, maybe, for when we live in spaces that are not places. When we cannot *go* home.

What is preserved and protected in these intense and vulnerable spaces, on-line and off-line, real and virtual and imagined, that we call home?

Memory and home are crucially interrelated. Gaston Bachelard writes (1964: 6, 15):

> Memories of the outside world will never have the same tonality as those of home and, by recalling these memories, we add to our store of dreams; we are never real historians, but always near poets, and emotion is perhaps nothing but an expression of a poetry that was lost.
>
> Thus by approaching the house with care not to break up the solidarity of memory and imagination, we may hope to make others feel all the psychological elasticity of an image that moves us at an unimaginable depth . . . the house shelters daydreaming, the house protects the dreamer, the house allows one to dream in peace. . . . The house we were born in is more than an embodiment of home, it is also an embodiment of dreams.

Home. The container of memory and cognition. The lives that have been led there, shared by families, both nuclear and extended, the familiarity of rooms and technologies, together provide a hold-all for the quotidian, its stories and its memories: of childhood, perhaps, above all. Our experiences of home are determined by the material circumstances of our everyday life, and by the ways in which they are remembered and recalled. Stories of home run like veins through the social body. And such stories are no longer innocent of media.

Think of your own childhood and adolescence, and think how often a musical fragment, a character in a soap opera narrative, or even the retelling of a major news event, summons up, like a perfume, a world. I think of mine. A black and white television screen in the front room. The

Coronation of Elizabeth II. Transistor radio under the pillow. The programmes of childhood: *Journey into Space, Two-way Family Favourites, The Cisco Kid, Quatermass and the Pit, In Town Tonight, The Six Five Special*, the Potter's Wheel, Radio Luxembourg. To share that world with one's contemporaries, to reflect on the past it evokes, is to connect with the other, to domesticate a shareable past. But it is also to include memories of media into one's own biography, into memories of home, good, bad and indifferent. These are the shaping experiences: of home as a mediated space, and of media as a domesticated space. Secure in them we can dream. Without them we are bereft. Within them certain kinds of understandings are possible: the taken-for-granted things of our everyday lives. Through them emerge private languages and personal moralities; the shared histories and identities of those who claim a singular dream of home.

Or desire it. Or project such dreams of worlds that have been lost into fantasy and longing. The media here too are central. For with modernity came dislocation, and as if to compensate for such material dislocation, the movement of populations, the disintegration of households, came the media. From pulpit to newspaper, from carnival to cinema, from vaudeville to broadcasting: the *mass* media. Compensations for the loss of home, translating images and claims of home into public space, projecting them on to neighbourhood and nation.

Walter Benjamin's version of this movement is the privatization of the nineteenth-century bourgeois interior. Those immaculate and immaculately controlled domestic spaces in which the world was constructed and claimed. 'The drawing room was the box in a world theatre' (Benjamin, 1976: 176), a space from which to claim the images and the information of a public space, and at the same time to be able to decide what to exclude. For Raymond Williams (1974) the media responded to a second wave of bourgeois confidence as families moved from city to suburb. Once again privatization was the theme, as broadcasting systems emerged to enable the dispersal of populations: to link the private home to a public one; indeed to redefine home as a space in which broadcasting was essential, and to define a particular version of home as appropriate to the conduct of everyday life. Radio first, then television:

> Broadcasting means the rediscovery of the home. In these days when house and hearth have been largely given up in favour of a multitude of other interests and activities outside, with the consequent disintegration of family ties and affections, it appears that this new persuasion may to some extent reinstate the parental roof in its old accustomed place, for all will admit that this is, or should be, one of the greatest and best influences on life. (C.A. Lewis, 1942, quoted in Frith, 1983: 110)

And now? Homes are vulnerable to history. This is not part of Bachelard's equation but we can scarcely ignore it. And doors, as I have suggested, can be both opened and closed. Homes are political now. They need to be continually reinvented. And the media are mobilized, as with so many technologies, to come to the rescue of an institution that they themselves are seen to be undermining. What a punishing paradox.

And yet it is possible to suggest that almost all our regulatory impulses, those that engage with the ownership of media industries on the one hand and those that concern the welfare of the family on the other, are between them concerned with the protection of home. What links them, of course, is *content*: the images, sounds and meanings that are transmitted and communicated daily, and over which governments feel they have increasingly little control. Content is important because it is presumed to be meaningful. Banal though it may seem, the media are seen to be important because of the power they are presumed to exercise over us, *at home*. They can breach the sanctuary as well as secure it. This is the struggle. This is the struggle over the family too; a struggle to protect it in its innocence and in its centrality as an institution where public and private moralities are supposed to coincide. This is a struggle for control, a struggle which propagandists and advertisers understood and still understand. And it is a struggle which parents understand too, as they argue with their children over their viewing habits or the time spent on-line, and which in part defines, across lines of age and gender, the particular politics of individual households.

Research conducted under the direction of George Gerbner (1986) at the University of Pennsylvania over a number of years suggests that those who watch television more intensely, an activity they define as 'mainstreaming', begin to articulate a view of their world that is uniquely television's own, representing, as it does, that world in terms at some remove from the realities of their daily lives. The world is seen through television's lens as it were and, they argue, such mainstreaming viewers are more anxious, more fearful, more conservative as a result. Such findings are perhaps not so surprising once one recognizes that any dominant medium, with more or less consistent, that is ideological, messages, is likely to have an effect on those who consume it And television is seen here as a threat to home and hearth, at least in its present form. Such findings are grist to the mill of moral and media reformers for whom the media are the source of much, if not all, evil. However, such moral and methodological naïveté is unsustainable, especially now that our media space extends beyond the power of the broadcasters to control it, and beyond the capacity of television to define its terms of trade as well as reference. The regulation of content is beginning to look like an impossibility.

And so the politics of the media continues, even if the premises on which it is based are inadequate and contradictory. And such a politics is concerned above all with the power to open and close doors, to control the rights of passage. It is concerned with control of trade routes and gateways, with set-top decoder technologies and encryption. It is concerned with cross-media ownership and the power of global capitalism to dominate the newly digital airwaves. It is concerned with the capacity of media to make or break life at home, to preserve national and domestic cultures, to enable the cultivation of that sense of place without which our humanity is vulnerable, a sense of location irrespective of where we might actually be.

And we study the media in its domesticity because of our general concern with the boundaries that surround that domesticity, and the particular threats that the screen, the electronic threshold, pose for us. The new ideology of interactivity, of course, one which stresses our capacity to extend reach and range and to control, through our own choices, what to consume, both when and how, is seen to promise its reversal. It is hailed to undo a century of one-to-many broadcasting and the progressive infantilization of an increasingly passive audience. It is an expression of a new millennialism. These are the utopian thoughts of the new age in which power is believed to have been given, at last, to the people: to the people, that is, who have access to, and can control, the mouse and the keyboard.

There are wider issues here, of course, and I will continue to pursue them, both in this section and in the remainder of the book. And in doing so I will attempt to hold within my own frame both the paradoxes of media power, and the capacity, equally paradoxical, of individuals in their daily lives to use the media to make sense of those lives, and to inform and articulate experience.

Home is where we start and where, in desire or reality, we end. The media engage and frame our sense of home, and enable us to mark the passages backwards and forwards, in time and in space. And this, arguably, is still the case, even in those societies and at those points in history, where home seems a lost cause: when populations are forced to flee; when whole cultures seem to stand on the edge of an abyss. We still need the myths of eternal return; and the media are one, key, source of those myths.

11 Community

We live among others. Therein lies our humanity. Therein also lies our capacity for inhumanity. We live in neighbourhoods, and in friendship and kinship groups. We live as members of ethnic majorities and minorities, as members of regions and nations. We share values and ideas and interests and beliefs and identify with those whose values, interests and beliefs are like our own. We share pasts as well as the immediate present: our biographies intertwined with histories and fused by memory. We find our identities in the social relations that are imposed upon us and those that we seek. We live them out on a daily basis. We have a sense of a need to belong. And we need reassurance that we do indeed belong. We construct ideas of what that thing to which we belong is, and we define and make sense of it in the images that we have of it, or in those that are offered to us. We need constantly to be reminded, reassured, that our sense of belonging and our involvement is worthwhile.

So we participate in activities that bring us together, activities that may have very little purpose other than to bring us together. Sometimes this sense of belonging is oppressive. The boundaries and the barriers that secure us also restrict us. Yet we hate to be excluded. We might leave one group one day only to join another the next. We distinguish ourselves from those who are different from us, and we create or find the symbols, from flags to football teams, to express those differences. Indeed such distinguishing is essential if we are to recognize and define our own distinctiveness. From time to time we do this quite aggressively: the necessity for distinction from others becomes a desire for the extinction of others. The differences are too hard to bear.

We call these contrary experiences of social life, 'community'. It is a descriptive and an evaluative term. One moment a benevolent and neutral observation about village life. The next a call to arms. One moment a framework for the analysis of the continuities and changes in social life. The next the heart of a lament for the loss of all that is perceived to be good and true.

We dream of community. Of the commonness and the shared realities that underpin it. We dream of a life with others; the security of place and familiarity and care. Indeed it is difficult to think of community without location; without a sense of the continuities of social life which are grounded, literally, in place. Community, then, is a version of home. But it is public not private. It is to be sought and sometimes found in the space between the household and the family and the wider society. Community always involves a claim. It is not just a matter of structure: of the institutions that enable participation and the organization of membership. It is also a matter of belief, of a set of claims to be part of something shareable and particular, a set of claims whose effectiveness is realized precisely and only in our acceptance of them. Communities are lived. But also imagined. And if people believe something to be real, then as the American sociologist W.I. Thomas famously noted, it is real in its consequences. Ideas of community hover between experience and desire.

When it comes to community, as Kobena Mercer (1996: 12) has noted, 'Everyone would like to be in one, but no-one is quite sure what it is.' This uncertainty is the product of a sense of loss but also the product of a sense of unease: that the world in which we now live, a world of fractured experience, fragmenting culture, and social and geographical mobility, has undermined and will continue to undermine our capacity to sustain social life meaningfully, securely and, perhaps above all, morally: in something, in other words, we wish to call community.

Where is it, this community? Where is it to be found now? On what does it depend: on what kinds of activities and personal and social commitments? How is community to be created and defended? Do we still want it? And how much does a sense of community, indeed the reality of community, depend upon our media, as agents of meaning, communication, participation, mobilization?

These are the questions that I want to pursue in this chapter. Community has become a buzz word. Embodied in the rhetorics of new and mostly conservative political movements, and in the rhetorics of public policy-makers at national and regional levels, it has become, often, an excuse for the absence of social thought. 'Care in the community' is a contradiction where there are no communities to care. The European Community is still a political fantasy. Communitarianism has become a creed premised on the assumption that there is no such thing as an intractable conflict on a moral or a political issue. And we are confronted too, and this is of course a central issue here, with the rhetorics of the information age, in which it is claimed that community, and with community some sense of identity and authenticity, can be found not in the world of face-to-face relationships (believed long destroyed by the relentless march of modernity) but in the displacements of the real by the electronic and the virtual: to move from off-line to on-line and then some.

New forms of social relationship, new forms of participation, new forms of citizenship, all seem possible in electronic space. We need to explore these claims and we need, too, to study how media and community have become so intensely and seductively intertwined.

The relationship between community and media is indeed a central one, and perhaps from the very beginning, with the emergence of a national press, the balance between the communities constructed through experience of the face-to-face, the continuities of an immobile society and the sharing of physical space and material culture, and those constructed through what we might call the imaginary, has been shifting. Benedict Anderson's discovery of the *imagined* community, created with the rise of the press and still constructed anew each day with the arrival and reading of the morning paper, describes the emergence of a shared symbolic space, the result of the simultaneous activity of the millions of individuals who in these acts of literary consumption align themselves with, and participate in, a national culture. The same news to be read each day and then forgotten: a mass ritual performed in 'the lair of the skull' (Anderson, 1983: 39, citing Hegel): the creation of an invisible public; the emergence of an abstract and abstracted community.

Vernacular mass printing enabled the formation of nation states, created around a shared language and an increasingly shareable culture. The newspaper intensified the process, the product as much as anything of the demands of a new imperial and industrial age, an age in which populations on the move needed a new basis for communication and culture, a new basis for belonging. So as physical boundaries became more porous and institutional constraints more lax, the ties that bind were increasingly to be sought, and indeed came to be found, in the realm of the symbolic.

Of course, communities have always been symbolic as well as material in their composition. They are defined through the minutiae of everyday interaction as well as through the effervescence of collective action. They are acted on and acted out. Yet without their symbolic dimension, they are nothing. Without their meanings, without belief, without identity and identification there is nothing: nothing in which to belong, in which to participate; nothing to share, nothing to promote, and nothing to defend. As Anthony Cohen (1985: 16) argues:

> The quintessential referent of community is that its members make, or believe they make, a similar sense of things either generally or with respect to specific and significant interests, and, further, that they think that that sense may differ from one made elsewhere. The reality of community in people's experience thus inheres in their attachment or commitment to a common body of symbols.

Communities are therefore defined not just by what is shared but by what is distinguished. And central to an understanding of community is the existence and nature, and power, of the boundaries that are drawn to distinguish one community from the next. Commonality and difference. But not necessarily uniformity. And no absolutes:

> The triumph of community is to so contain this variety [of behaviour and ideas] that its inherent discordance does not subvert the apparent coherence which is expressed by its boundaries. . . . The important thrust of this argument is that this relative similarity or difference is not a matter of 'objective' assessment: it is a matter of feeling, a matter which resides in the minds of the members themselves. (Cohen, 1985: 20)

Cohen makes this as a general argument relevant to community, not just to historically specific communities, yet it is hard not to believe that the capacity to make it at all, as well as its increasing relevance, is the product of a modern age in which, precisely and empirically, community has come to be constructed in the public texts and symbols of everyday life: in the mediated meanings of electronic culture.

Let me follow Cohen's argument further for doing so will take us into the heart of the questions that need to be raised about the media. Central is the issue of the boundary. And central too is the participation in ritual. Boundaries define and contain and distinguish. Within them individuals find shareable meanings and the symbols that come to *represent* community also have a powerful role in *defining* it. Rituals involve symbolic behaviour. We participate in activities which are pregnant with meaning. Rituals bind us, in our differences, together under an umbrella of a common but powerful set of images and ideas which are the mechanisms for asserting and reinforcing our uniqueness, and which allow us to distinguish ourselves from those, our neighbours, whose way of life we wish to distance and exclude. Rituals are essential to community, and community, in its expression and reflection in ritual, is essentially a claim for difference. Awareness of the symbolic boundaries of our culture and their dramatization in their performance is a precondition for the making and holding of community. Our boundaries define us. We study the media because they provide a constant resource for community, though, as I shall suggest, in sometimes unexpected and contradictory ways.

Indeed, the media *do* community in three ways: expression, refraction and critique. It might even be possible to suggest that these three dimensions of media and community are both historically and technologically specific. I will come back to this.

Benedict Anderson's perception of the role of the press in creating an imagined community on a national scale is an example of the way in which the media could be seen to express community. But in an age of radio and television this capacity and the claims that have been made for it extend beyond the range and reach of the printed word. Radio, that is public service broadcast radio, was the national community-building medium *par excellence*. The Treaty of Versailles marked a watershed in the status of the nation in Europe, and the post-war period saw the emergence, for better and ill, of both ideologies and institutions dedicated to the construction of strong and singular national communities.

Radio became a crucial part of this, and self-consciously so. The BBC, under John Reith, pursued the vision perhaps most benignly. Hitler's use of the radio was, of course, another story. Yet both saw in radio the capacity to provide the symbolic raw materials with which a nation could build a shareable identity. And radio did this not just through the appeal to dispersed and anonymous audiences, but in the transmission for that audience of a range of schedules, narratives and highly charged events that together provided, for those who were willing to listen, the symbolic framework for participation in the community. To believe in it and to act on its behalf. BBC programming provided structure, in the cycle of the daily and weekly schedules and the live broadcasting of major national rituals, both sacred and secular; and it provided content in the programmes that told the nation's tales, reformed its myths and its histories, transmitted its sounds and its voices. Coronations, cup finals, conversations; music and talk; the nightly news bulletin; the turgid, the trivial and the transcendent; something for everyone.

The singularity and consistency of radio's address, even in its variation, was a precise expression of, and claim for, community. In war-time – when the gloves came, and still come, off – it is transparent. Ideology is replaced by propaganda. The community must be mobilized. But in the early years, and now, the broadcast media have been able to provide, discretely for the most part, though not always necessarily entirely successfully, the social glue that is community. This was and is the nation expressing itself, creating and sustaining itself, defining itself in its uniqueness and its difference. The boundary is both linguistic and technical: English the language, the United Kingdom the territory and the limit of transmission. But the boundary is also defined, and of course defended, in the creation of a symbolic reality, in the presumption of its relevance and in the pursuit of its power.

The boundaries of community can also be defined in other ways, and media are central here too. Whereas in the media's *expression* of community one can detect a singular political agenda as well as a social one, and one can see, in these claims for community, a direct appeal for identification and participation, the *experience* of community is less direct, and community is *refracted* in often less than obvious ways.

Anthony Cohen draws attention to the phenomenon of symbolic reversal, the ways in which:

> people not only mark a boundary between their community and others, but also reverse or invert the norms of behaviour and values which 'normally' mark their own boundaries. In these rituals of reversal, people behave quite differently and collectively in ways which they supposedly abhor or which are usually proscribed. (Cohen, 1985: 58)

There is a huge agenda here. Perhaps the best way to deal with it is to return to Jerry Springer. The man and his show are reviled. Yet they are intensely watched. And they have spawned huge numbers of imitators. US day-time TV is wall-to-wall confessional and the virus is spreading. As a particular expression of the depths to which popular culture will descend it has few equals, and yet it is precisely that descent which is the issue.

Popular culture has always had the capacity for reversal. Carnival was merely its most visible expression. Societies have been contained, and communities have been sustained, through the often clearly bounded rituals in which it became possible to perform and proclaim all that was antagonistic to what was dominant or presumed to be dominant in the culture of the times. Transgression and transcendence involved descent and reversal, and as long as it did not get out of hand it was tolerated, and indeed encouraged. For an anthropologist such moments and events are profoundly functional. The Lords of Misrule ruled and in their proclamations perversely reinforced the power of the symbolic and of the hold that the community had on its members; and the power of the ritual enabled the members of that community to identify in the mirror with the obverse of what it was that made them different and special. An experience to be shared and dramatized. Meanings to be sustained. A sense of belonging.

In our own mass-mediated times the popular is still at work, and this ritual function, in which the values and ideas of a community are reflected in reverse, is still sustained. Put to one side for the moment a critique which would see this as a deliberate strategy of a dominant capitalism and totalitarian society, and consider what might be going on and its relevance for an understanding of community.

There are historical and cultural continuities between the popular press and the latest manifestations of popular television. The tabloids and the yellow press did not even begin it. Printing spawned a scurrilous and seditious vernacular literature just as it produced the religious and the intellectual. And what these various manifestations of the popular provided was a location for boundary definition in which dominant values were continually being transgressed and subverted, but in that very process were, mostly, affirmed. Classes and cultures found their distinctiveness in such texts and symbolic manifestations of community. In such places and at such times it became possible to do and say things that would be otherwise unacceptable but which were structurally related to what was acknowledged as the specifically normal. In such places and at such times it became possible to play and to perform against the grain, and in the sharing of that play and in those performances, solidarity was asserted and claimed both within the playing group and within the community as a whole. Though, of course, the popular was not just a site for containment but a stimulus for social and cultural change.

What is going on, on Springer, if not the ritual proclamation through personal testimony and dramatic interpersonal conflict of the unsaid and unsayable in social life? What is being displayed on Springer is incest and infidelity, transsexuality and transgressions of all kinds. They are being played out through highly ritualized conflicts in front of an invited and participating audience, and for the most part the players are from the underclass of modern society: urban blacks, poor Southern whites, second-generation Hispanics whose own cultures are denied and repressed and who have been offered and claimed this space for their own version of misrule.

Boundaries are being both transgressed and in transgression affirmed here. The space for reversal is tightly defined, not just by the framing of the time available for each show, but through Springer's own concluding homily in which the abnormal is either restored to or justified against dominant forms of reality, those values and beliefs that he expects his audience to understand and to share. There is actually not much left to chance. And it is in the expectation that the audience will understand the relationship between what they see and what they know that some sense of community is being claimed. Here is community reflected through the media lens. Here, I am suggesting, boundaries around our culture are being defined and reinforced and here too, in ways that we may find hard to take, the media are also providing a glimpse of a changing world.

The third way in which the media 'do' community, which I want briefly to consider, concerns the media's role as critic. Again there is nothing new in the ways in which media have been able to engage critically in the political or ethical frameworks that sustain the communities within which they appear. No boundary is sacrosanct. Yet through both the rapid expansion of community radio and the growth of the Internet it is possible to see, ironically in both the oldest and the newest of mass media, a freedom to pursue a critical or alternative agenda, from the margins, as it were, or from the underbelly of social life. Community radio has a significant role in the developing world in this regard, and in advanced industrial societies the release of spectrum and the digitalization of communication have created new spaces for alternative voices that provide the focus both for specific community interests as well as for the contrary and the subversive.

As a result of these developments, the minority and the local, the critical and the global, it is possible to suggest that the first and most significant casualty will be the national community.

Consider for a moment the case of ethnic minority television in the coming age of digital satellite and cable transmission, an age in which, in principle at least, there will be fewer limits on access to broadcast channels and where the price of entry will also be, relatively, low. A report published in 1998 (Silverstone, 1998) made a case for the creation of a Jewish cable or satellite channel in the UK. The argument was based on the particular characteristics and perceived needs of the Jewish community in the UK, a community with a history of assimilative participation in the culture of the host society, but one now riven by discord and demographic decline. The report suggested that the Jewish community could be revived, its secular culture invigorated, by the creation of just such a channel. Within it Jewish voices would be heard and Jewish values and ideas would be discussed. This was perceived as an opportunity for expression and reflection. But it was one being claimed by a minority. Other ethnic minorities had already been, or would soon be, doing the same.

These claims for community through the media are critical, but in two senses. They offer an alternative vision of broadcasting's role in the community, and they offer an alternative vision of community. The new claims are for participation and closer links between the on-line/off-line of broadcast space. But the claims are also for communities in the plural: discrete, arguably inward-looking, and likely to have powerful repercussions on the quality and character of public life in the next century. There are clearly unresolved tensions here. They involve contradictory versions of community in both the structure and content of media, and the character and consequence of the media's role in the general texture of experience.

Here is certainly an agenda for those of us who wish to study media. Community may well be an over- and mis-used term, but it addresses some of the core questions of what it is that makes daily life both possible and acceptable. The familiar bases for the creation and maintenance of community throughout modernity are beginning to erode. In this, media are central, for they provide the symbolic resources for both change and resistance to change.

However, the agenda is not exhausted in a concern with minority broadcasting or community radio. There is a global agenda too for community, and a new medium to create and sustain it. Enter the virtual community and social life on the Internet.

One by-product of my argument in this chapter is the recognition that *all communities are virtual communities*. The symbolic expression and definition of community, both with or without electronic media, has been established as a *sine qua non* of our sociability. Communities are imagined and we participate in them both with and without the face-to-face, both with and without touch. Those who proclaim a new age of community made possible by the Internet argue that community is possible without propinquity, and that through persistent multiple communications (sometimes, as in Harold Rheingold's 1994 account of the WELL, supported by subsequent and possibly intensely deflating face-to-face interactions) among a self-selecting group of (English language-writing) enthusiasts a shared social reality is created, one in which individuals are supported and in which they can both find meaning and express and sustain a personal identity.

It is not my intention, and it would seem to me to be rather pointless, to pursue the question of whether these new mediated fora are 'real' communities or not. It is equally not my intention to pursue, item by item, the ways in which sustainable social interaction as well as collective fantasy are possible in the MUDs and Usenet groups that dominate computer-mediated communication. Quite clearly, in the latter case, however depressed those involved have been argued to be (Kraut et al., 1998), there is every reason to believe that sustainable sociability of a sort is possible. These really are questions for further study.

Yet it is clear that there are major issues still to be resolved, not least at the interface between on-line and off-line 'communities', and in the capacity of new expressions of electronic sociability to compensate for the perceived failures of traditionally mediated sociability. This is particularly the case, as I have suggested, in relation to the new media's role in public life, and in their capacity to enable meaningful participation in the political process. I will return to these issues in my final chapter.

12 Globe

Thomas Wolfe's magisterial novel, *Of Time and the River*, is dominated by the image and the metaphor of the train. Symbol of modernity and of the restlessness of youth, it drives the narrative ever onwards, into new lands, new times, into America and into America's century. The story begins with a train journey, from the South to the North. Later there is another one. Only this time a race between trains from rival companies. Neck and neck they run alongside each other, one pulling slightly ahead, then the next. Eugene Gant watches from the warm, secure interior of his Pullman car, and sees the passengers in the other train, as they see him:

> And they looked at one another for a moment, they passed and vanished and were gone for ever, yet it seemed to him that he had known these people, that he knew them better than the people in his own train, and that, having met them for an instant under immense and timeless skies, as they were hurled across the continent to a thousand destinations, they had met, passed, vanished, yet would remember this for ever. And he thought the people in the two trains felt this, also: slowly they passed each other now, and their mouths smiled and their eyes grew friendly, but he thought there was some sorrow and regret in what they felt. For, having lived together as strangers in the immense and swarming city, they now had met upon the everlasting earth, hurled past each other for a momenc between two points in time upon the shining rails, never to meet, to speak, to know each other any more, and the briefness of their days, the destiny of man, was in that instant greeting and farewell. (Wolfe, 1971: 473)

Wolfe published this in 1935. It was set in the 1920s.

The railway arguably began it: a new communication technology opening up continents for ordinary folk, defining the particular character of our own modernity, that peculiar and paradoxical imbalance of movement and stasis, of recognition and alienation, of place and placelessness, of time and timelessness, of connection and disconnection, of the fragile and the ephemeral, of gain and of loss.

Transport and communication. Travel, trade and empire. Railway, telegraph, telephone, radio, film, television, the Internet, drawing modernity and globalization together: from steam to valves to transistors to chips. A continuous process of domination, extension and abstraction, as technology progressively shrinks the globe. What we now define as globalization and what we now herald as a brave new world released by the wonders of the electronic and digital has a history. A history of the machine, a history of the institutions and industries that grew up around the machine and a history of the things, the people, the news, the images, the ideas, the values, that were transmitted by the machine. And because globalization has a history we need to be cautious in ascribing it exclusively to the post-modern condition.

To some extent globalization is a state of mind; it extends as far as the imagination. Maps of the world, in their various projections, have always offered representations of what is known and believed and claimed to be within reach. We all have our own maps of the world and of our place within them.

But globalization is also a material reality. Industry, finance, economy, polity, culture, all both separately and together operate on, and are constructed within, global space and global time: transgressing boundaries, transcending identities, fracturing communities, universalizing images. And the media both enable and represent this process. So much so that we increasingly take it for granted. We take it for granted that our telephone calls and e-mails reach the other side of the world in seconds, that images of live catastrophes and football matches, and dead day-time soap operas, can be seen on screens in every city on the planet. And we take it for granted that, as Joshua Meyrowitz once noted, 'Television . . . now escorts children across the globe even before they have permission to cross the street' (Meyrowitz, 1985: 238).

Undoubtedly we live in a global age. The world, literally, is our oyster. It is an age in which time–space relations are to be replaced by space–time relations, in which history retreats in the face of geography and geography no longer needs material space to justify its existence. Harold Innes, Marshall McLuhan's mentor, saw these changes as being a direct result of changes in the nature of communication. McLuhan did too, and presciently but inaccurately coined the phrase the 'global village' to describe what he thought he saw. And after him, James Carey and Walter Ong, together, provided a framework within the study of the media, which placed technological change at the heart of the matter. Our capacity to connect, to communicate, to inform, to entertain, instantly, insistently and intensely anywhere and everywhere has profound consequences for our place in the world, and our capacity to understand it. Here, now, if we have not already had one, is a reason for studying the media, for its role in all of this, in its enabling and in its transforming of social and cultural relations on the world stage, and in its significance for us as we go about our daily business in that world.

Globalization is the product of a changing economic and political order, one in which technology and capital have combined in a new multi-faceted imperialism. We might be cautious in insisting on capitalism's capacity for infinite expansion, and we would certainly recognize its destructive force when it comes to community. Yet despite the visible shredding round the edges, in Malaysia, in Russia and South America as the millennium is approached, its post-war history is one of extraordinary success. It is impossible to ignore the imbalances and inequities that mark the global economy, but it is equally impossible to ignore its capacity for reproduction and continuous expansion.

The past half-century has seen transformation in the productive capacity of global capitalism. The shift from a national, Fordist, to an international, post-Fordist, economy has brought the manufacturing and distributing process closer to the consumer: more responsive, increasingly demand driven, with different attitudes to labour and major consequences for the industrialization of the world. There are those who describe the shift as one from organized to disorganized capitalism. Capital, however, now operates on a world stage in a way that was impossible to conceive even a few years ago: shifting commodities, shifting labour, shifting plant from one region to another with little consideration for the needs of local economies or the desires of national governments. Always just in time. There is a touching belief in the rationality of all of this, yet the most obvious consequences – the incapacity of nations to understand their economies, let alone control them; the social costs generated by the consequent insecurities of employment; and the increasingly vulnerable financial and economic global interdependencies – have produced a world increasingly on edge.

Those who argue for free trade, in nuts and bolts as well as music and movies, tend to dominate that trade, and in the post-war world capitalism and globalization have gone hand in hand; they both require each other. Enabling both, of course, is the free and instant flow of information, a flow which requires a new economics for its understanding and control, a flow which has had profound consequences for the way organizations operate in time and space, a flow which many believe will have profound consequences, in turn, for the identity of individual cultures and societies and their capacity to survive.

The cultural industries were some of the first to globalize: both cause and consequence of the shrinking planet. Hollywood is still the paradigm. So when we talk, as we do and as I will go on to do here, of the kinds of freedoms still to be had for minority cultures and local interests both to contribute to, or appropriate, global culture, we still have to remind ourselves, do we not, of the terms under which the trade is conducted. We still have to note the scale and scope of control exercised within the cultural industries by the multinational, even if its headquarters is Berlin, Tokyo or London rather than Atlanta or Seattle. And even if we note, as again we must, the lack of precise coincidence between ownership and content, the equation does not always work out in favour of diversity and openness. Sony do not, by and large, produce Japanese culture for the globe. They produce the culture of Hollywood and what was once called tin-pan alley. There is very little left of the global commons. It has nearly all been enclosed.

My concern here is with globalization as a mediated cultural force and with its relationship to experience. Our perception of our place in the world, of course, is dependent on how we live in it as well as how we see it. In this respect I hazard to suggest that we are constantly moving in and out of global culture. We move from local frames of reference, the ordinariness of the everyday, the neighbourhood, the local, into the times and spaces that have a more extensive reference and definition. We do that in both our work and leisure. We do it in both physical and symbolic space. We do it willingly and under threat. And in those movements, the movements of individuals and groups, we are constantly claiming the right to be ourselves, claiming identity, claiming a share of what little, indeed, is left of the global commons. Trespassers, poachers, terrorists, all. And sometimes successfully so.

Writers have identified this as a process of reverse flow: from the local and the individual to the global and the collective instead of the other way around. They point to the capacity of local cultures, most often and especially, musical cultures, to extend into global space and to change it. They point to the symbolic power exercised by the Bombay film industry or the Brazilian tele-novella. Flow is, however, probably a misnomer. Trickle might be closer to the mark, and even then not without a struggle, and not without a constant shift of meaning. The music of Soweto as expressed in the *mbube* of Ladysmith Black Mambazo entered global space with Paul Simons's now classic appropriation of it on his *Graceland* album. All the ambiguities and contradictions of such a move are visible here: a permanent charge on, and change within, global popular music culture; the visibility of minority voices and harmonies in the same culture, yet a transformation of meaning and significance once those voices leave the township. And one can ask too what effects such global visibility has on the local music and its capacity to maintain what we might be naïve enough to want to call its authenticity.

Indeed, in what Arjun Appadurai (1996) calls the *mediascape*, globalization is a process of translation. We believe that financial information transmitted instantly between London and Hong Kong or Singapore is the same when it arrives as when it leaves. We believe that Hollywood or Disney is the same in Paris or Penang as it is in Poughkeepsie. We believe that the news of the world is the same wherever it is received. But we know that it is not. We know that meanings travel far and fast but they travel neither innocently nor invulnerably. We know that satellite pictures transmitted live from the Gulf during war-time tell one story here and quite another there, and that the story will change in both places in time. And as I have just suggested, we know that cultures, local cultures, minority cultures, increasingly defensive aggressive cultures, have the capacity, still, to work with the meanings that come from elsewhere, and also to contribute to them.

What does the global mean to the different groups and cultures which exist within it? There is a tension here: between the forces of homogenization and fragmentation; between bland acceptance and resistance; between consumption and expression; between fear and favour. The hybrid cultures that are formed both in the centre and the periphery of the world system, cultures still significantly shaped by national cultural policies, emerge at all levels. And we, for these are our cultures, are confronted by a constant interplay of identity and difference. One minute Diet Coke, the next chopped liver.

Generalization becomes impossible or, if not impossible, not terribly interesting. The fragile unity of the world economic order is automatically expressed neither in a uniform political order nor in a cultural one. Those who talk of space–time distanciation, or space–time compression, as the common denominator of the global, and find in either or both an ontological underpinning, as well as an undermining, of our capacity to the live in the world, offer too great an abstraction. The disembedding, 'the "lifting out" of social relations from local contexts of interaction across indefinite spans of space-time' (Giddens, 1990: 27), has a long history in modernity on the one hand (as the extract from Thomas Wolfe illustrates), but it is by no means, even now, a uniform global experience. Consider the number of telephones, television sets and computers per head of population in Soweto, or even the capacity of the ordinary man and woman there to participate meaningfully in the global economy, and reflect on what the global might mean, in its variations and in its difference.

No. We study the media because we need to recognize both the ambiguities and contradictions of global culture and global cultures. And we also study the media because we need to know how global cultures actually work. We also need to know what needs to be done to preserve and enhance minority interests. In what sense do we actually live in global culture and in what ways do the media enable or disable us from doing so?

I want to pursue this question in relation to the media's role among groups disadvantaged or marginalized by mainstream culture, minorities whose place in global culture and society is defined, both positively and negatively, by their dislocation, by their participation in what has been recognized as one of the key dimensions of social life in the late twentieth century: the diaspora.

The diaspora was once singular. It described the dispersion of Jews after the fall of the second temple in Jerusalem, a dispersion which took them to the far corners of what was then the globe: into North Africa, Iberia, India and to Europe, both East and West. Diaspora is now plural. It describes the multiple movements of global populations across the globe. The end of the Second World War found millions of people displaced across Europe. Since then that movement has become continental, as populations and cultures have moved from one locality to others, pulled by opportunities of work or other advantage, pushed by poverty, famine or political unrest.

To say that these populations have somehow been absorbed, assimilated, into either their host or even a uniform global culture would be, for the most part, an obvious error. Indeed contemporary global politics is in significant measure a politics in which minorities, recently or less recently displaced, are seeking, and seeking to defend, not just the right to exist materially but the right to maintain their own culture, their own identity. Again this can be, and has been, both benign and malign in its consequences. But what unites these various activities is the sense that the populations that are involved are both local and global at the same time: they are local in so far as they are minority cultures living in particular places, but they are global in their range and reach. Not so much communities, more like networks: networks linking members in different spaces, in different cities, networks linking the dispersed with those who have remained, in some sense of the term, at home. Networks that are, indeed, increasingly operating through media. Displaced populations, Punjabis in Southall, Moroccan Jews in Bordeaux, Turks in Berlin, Albanians in Milan, Mexicans in Sacramento, Chinese in Toronto, Greeks in Melbourne, Irish in Boston, Cubans in Miami, can maintain links with other similarly displaced groups around the world, and also with their country of origin.

In a short but suggestive essay, exploring the mechanics and implications of this process and what he calls 'interdiasporic media', Daniel Dayan (1998) lists the various traditional and what he calls 'neo-traditional' ways in which dispersed groups can and do maintain their own version of global culture. These range from the production and circulation of newsletters, audio-cassettes and video-cassettes (both commercially and domestically produced), holy icons and other small media to the exchange of letters, telephone calls, photographs and individual travellers, and the constitution of interdiasporic networks by religious or political organizations with specific agendas. And this is without mentioning their participation in the major mass media which provide, increasingly through cable and satellite delivery, global access to local programming, both in television and radio, and of course through the Internet.

These are each manifestations of particular media enabling global networks to form. The result? A degree of connection. The impossibility of exile. The capacity of minorities anywhere to be minorities everywhere. The capacities of cultures to survive, perhaps, when they might not otherwise do so, though inevitably transformed in the process. There are questions here, of course, related to the passage of time and to the different experiences of first, second and subsequent generations of migrants; to the use of different media and their role in enabling the formation and re-formation of minority cultures in the contrary spaces of host societies and global frames. From this point of view globalization is a multifaceted and, above all, a contested process. Not the exclusive preserve of elites, nor of the global media, but a to-ing and fro-ing of identities and interests, mobilized and articulated through an increasingly electronic space, but still dependent on, and vulnerable to, the real movements of diverse populations through space and time.

Minorities have to negotiate their difference in both local and global contexts. The media provide resources for that: both the media that they generate and the media that they receive; the media of their own culture and that of their host culture. What emerges, of course, is something new: a minor cosmopolitanism, a new shifting hybridity, reflected and expressed in the media, both old and new. This is Marie Gillespie concluding her study of media and identity among the South Asian diaspora in West London:

> as the globalisation of communications and cultures articulates new kinds of temporal and spatial relations, it transforms the modes of identification available within societies. Media are being used by productive consumers to maintain and strengthen boundaries, but also to create new, shared spaces in which syncretic cultural forms, such as 'new ethnicities', can emerge. These processes are uneven and their consequences unforeseeable, though likely to be weighty. But they cannot be examined in the abstract or at a distance. (Gillespie, 1995: 208–9)

In all these senses globalization is a dynamic process. The connections are there to be made. Cultures form and re-form around the different stimuli that global communications enable. Gillespie's study draws out the role of television and particularly video in enabling the first-generation parental immigrants to maintain links with their countries and cultures of origin, somehow, albeit at many removes, keeping in touch with tradition; while the same media allow their children to relocate, to redefine a cultural space where the *Mahabharata*, *EastEnders*, and MTV coincide.

Of course, globalization is contradictory in its effects as well as its meanings. When Kenneth Starr placed his report to the US Congress on the Internet for the world to see, and then to be reproduced on the front pages and the television screens of the world's media, he went instantly global, as if somehow there was a global jury to which to appeal. Taxi drivers in every city of the world would be asking their passengers their views. It would become global gossip. If this is what McLuhan meant by the global village, then maybe he had a point. An event shared. Yet in its drawing down into the bowels of national, local, regional, ethnic, religious, private cultures, its meanings and its significance fragment. From the Taliban to Trinidad, one cannot presume a consistency of interpretation. Nor can one assume that the singularity of the event, its global presence, will somehow generate a uniform response. The *topic* may be global, but it becomes a *resource* for the expression of local and particular interests and identities.

And so we might ask, what happens to this sense of the global when it is confronted by our everyday experience? How can I, do I, understand my place in this global world? How much can I bear of it? How much responsibility can I take? Or, more to the point, how much am I being asked to take? How deep does it go, this globalization? Is it itself an 'as-if' of media representation? Does it depend on the crucial, and untimely, separation of culture from society?

To ask these questions is of course to raise a set of moral and political questions that cannot be simply answered, though I will discuss them again in the final section of this book. But it is to pose the globalization question in the reverse of its usual formulation. For media-driven globalization is seen by many as the foundation for a global politics, for global citizenship, for, indeed, a global society. Television and, above all, the Internet provide the global space for global traffic in images, ideas and beliefs that can be, manifestly, shared. As if to see and hear is to understand. As if information is knowledge. As if access is participation. As if participation is effectiveness. As if communities of interest can replace interesting communities. As if global chat, both the synchronous and asynchronous, is communication.

We travel, like Wolfe's passengers, on a global infrastructure, passing each other like thieves in the night. Moments of recognition, moments of identification. Ephemeral connections to distant events and lives. Some we claim. Some we mobilize. Some we keep at arm's length. Events occurring across the planet are seen and discussed on our screens. From time to time they affect us deeply. They may be seen to require a response: a gift, a donation to charity, the purchase of an extra newspaper. And there are things there for us to learn, for us to take home. Internet sites, home pages, for the weary cyber-traveller. There are votes to cast and views to express, and there is power still to be exercised.

The global is a fragile thing. The global economy is holding itself together by the skin of its teeth. The global polity is yet stillborn. Global culture is seen but not often heard. States survive. Regionalism advances. Social conflicts are endemic. Yet, and there is always a yet, our imagination encompasses the globe in ways that are both new and tangible. The media enable this, for they provide the raw material for that imaginative work. What remains at issue is how the imaginary can be fixed on the canvases of everyday life and, once again, what role the media might have in that endeavour. This is the topic of my next section.

Making sense

This section is about making sense and fixing meanings. In it I pursue the media's centrality for our capacity to create and sustain order in our daily lives and for our capacity to find and position ourselves within that order. The media have become indispensable to that enterprise. Our media literacy creates a context in which both reference and reflection, the constant iterations of common sense and the defining characteristics of modernity, must themselves be referred to in the media's own ubiquitous presence and representation. Once we can read, how can we ignore the book?

Order and disorder are temporal, spatial and social. Classification involves the measure of difference and similarity, in time and in space, and by degree. Cultures and individuals are both involved. Our common sense and our commonplaces are our touchstones of reality: where our order is to be found and justified. The media are, in significant degree, the raw material, the tools, but also the product of our work with those tools: together, the sand, the spade, the castle and the flag of everyday life. In that sense the media are, essentially, reflexive. And in that sense, too, we would be lost without them.

But the media's project is not without irony, and not without contradiction. Deeply ingrained in the fabric of the social order as it is, it provides both a route to, and a barrier against, reality. Our lives in the mass-mediated subjunctive world require constant reassurance. The texture of experience, that which informs and supports our actions, needs continuous attention. The truth and validity of what we see and hear, and what we feel, has to be tested, constantly tested. There are, always, distortions and irresolvable conflicts. There are things we don't see clearly, and things that mislead. We need to understand this, to understand how the media contribute to our inhabited certainties and uncertainties, as individuals and as members of the social world.

The key dimensions of the social process, those that locate us in space, time and identity, those that enable us to manage risk, history and the presence of others, are no longer, if they ever were, ones that were innocent of mediation. Our conceptual and imaginative reach is boundless, and this is of course perceived as both a liberation and a constraint. The reach into history, the reach across continents is, as I have already suggested on many occasion, a reach which transforms as it captures. Tradition conflicts with translation. Identity with community. Sense with sensibility.

What follows is an exploration of three dimensions of the media's capacity to provide a framework for the conduct of social life and for the pursuit of security and identity within the everyday. Trust, memory, otherness: each is central to that basic social project and each is crucially defined and inflected in our relationships to the media, in all their aspects. Each involves the creation and maintenance of value, and, implicitly, it is the question of value that I am asking. I am, therefore, after something perhaps quite intangible, but something which, in its way, is the most fundamental of all. It is a perception of the media as being one of the root formations of modern society, deeply embedded in, and powerfully affecting, our humanity.

13 Trust

I click onto Amazon.com, the Internet bookstore. 'Safe and easy ordering – guaranteed!' A page of reassurance. I will never need to worry about credit-card safety, since every transaction will be 100 per cent safe. I am protected against any unauthorized charges. The combination of Amazon's guarantee and the US Fair Credit Billing Act limits my own liability to $50 and Amazon will cover me for anything up to that, 'if the unauthorised use of (my) credit card resulted through no fault of (my) own' (though presumably only if the transaction takes place in the US). I am assured that there is safety in numbers: over 3 million customers have safely shopped with Amazon without credit-card fraud. And I am assured that the technology is safe. Secure Server Software (SSL), the industry standard, encrypts all my personal information so that it cannot be read as 'the information travels over the Internet'. If I am still worried all I have to do is enter the last five numbers of my credit card and I will be given instructions on ordering by phone. Am I reassured? What is going on here?

I am being asked to trust an abstract system. I am being told that my money will be safe and my identity will be protected. No one will know what I'm ordering. No money of mine will disappear into the wrong hands. I am being asked to put my faith in technology. I am told that the federal government will protect me from the worst. And I am being offered a reassuring metaphor of the process: that the information that I have provided is actually travelling safely across a network.

I can, because I'm old enough, construct in my mind's eye an electronic version of those containers travelling through vacuum tubes in the department stores of what now seems like another age: folded money speeding to its destination, the counting house on the sixth floor, and then returning with a hand-written receipt. Whoosh! Nothing too problematic in that. Neither then nor now. And even if there is, even if somehow the absence of a person or a voice in the electronic transaction, the lack of an acknowledgement of my own humanity and identity, a failure to recognize that I may be something more than simply an abstraction myself, even if these are still troubling, then I can telephone. I can return to a technological infrastructure with which I am familiar (though which I may once have distrusted too). I can deliver my voice to a recording machine, and somehow draw the sting of suspicion.

But if I still distrust? If somehow my sense of the whole process is still conditioned not by metaphors of safety but of chaos, by visions of lines being crossed, and of packages disappearing into the ether, like my office assistant on Microsoft Office '97 when I decide to click it off. If I have no sense of a destination, or of north and south. If I believe not at all in the solidity and security of the electronic word. Or if I imagine, on the contrary, an intense information system cross-tabulating every single electronic transaction I have ever made, with the result that I will start receiving targeted junk mail seeking to get me to buy more stuff. If I imagine that I am being reconstructed as some kind of cyber-me in electronic space: a digital consumer, all bits and bytes and incriminating evidence, to be sold on to the next supplier of commercial or political information. If I have found myself, in the past, struggling incomprehensibly with telephone bills which always seem to be double what I imagine they should be. If I have failed to make the transition from one technology to another. If the new is unfamiliar and threatening. If I still wish to cling to the securities of the face-to-face, and the dust of my local bookshop. If I still need to touch to transact. What then?

I cannot be made to trust. Trust is not an act of will. On the contrary. Trust is both a precondition for, and a consequence of, such a transaction as I might make with Amazon.com, or any other continuous or regular transactions with a bank, a supermarket or a travel agent. Or indeed with any other actor in my social space. And trust, in this intensely mediated world, is both undermined and restored by the media themselves. Here, as elsewhere, the media are central; not just in their capacity to represent actions and interactions as trustworthy and in those representations reassure, but in their intimate participation in communication, at the interface where trust is, or is not, enabled. Trust, as Partha Dasgupta (1988: 50) remarks, is a fragile commodity.

Without trust we could not survive. As social, economic or political beings. Trust is essential for the management of everyday life; for our own sense of personal security in a complex world; for our capacity to act, to get on with each other, to share, to co-operate, to belong. How do we manage it? What role do the media play in that management? What can studying the media tell us about the creation and sustaining of trust in our global world?

And what is trust?

> trusting a person means believing that when offered the chance, he or she is not likely to behave in a way that is damaging to us, and trust will *typically* be relevant when at least one party is free to disappoint the other, free enough to avoid a risky relationship, *and* constrained enough to consider the relationship an attractive option. In short, trust is implicated in most human experience, if of course to widely different degrees. (Gambetta, 1988: 219)

Thus the economist Diego Gambetta. Trust becomes significant when I have to make a judgement about someone else's behaviour towards me under conditions when I cannot monitor what they have done before. For trust to be relevant, there must be a possibility for others to betray us. Trust is a device for coping with the freedom of others.

Basic trust has its source in the experience of childhood; indeed, in the earliest experiences of childhood. The British psychoanalyst D.W. Winnicott has developed a theory of the individual which places at its centre an explanation of the capacity to feel and to be secure in the world. 'Ontological security', once again both the precondition and the consequence of our ability to trust, emerges as a result of the consistencies of care that a parent provides for a child in the first months of infancy, and the consequent development of the kind of confidence in oneself as well as in others that is the result of such care.

Ontological security is a condition which is grounded in, and is in turn enabling of, our being in the world. We learn, unconsciously, and if we are lucky enough, to trust our early surroundings and especially those who people them. We learn to distinguish ourselves from others, to test the boundary between fantasy and reality, to begin the long process which will enable us to contribute to the society in which we live, through the consistencies of care and attention which we receive. Such trust keeps anxiety at bay. It allows us to manage what otherwise would be an eternally threatening complex world in which all interactions would have to be dealt with as if they were the first, in which experience would count for nothing and in which we would not be able to distinguish reality, honesty and good intentions from their obverse.

For most of us, most of the time, our natural attitude in the taken-for-granted world is the one which enables us to maintain our sanity in our passage through life and the daily round. Routines, habits, cognitive and emotional reinforcements, continually reaffirmed, the often highly ritualized securities of our passage through time and space, and the consistencies with which our interactions with each other conform to expectations, together provide the infrastructure for a moral universe in which we, its citizens, can go about our daily business. Through learning to trust others we learn, one way or another, to trust things. And, likewise, through learning to trust material things we learn to trust abstract things. Trust is therefore achieved and sustained through the ordinariness of everyday life and the consistencies of both language and experience.

But such trust has to be continually worked for, just as our participation in everyday life requires an ongoing commitment. We have to do both:

> what is learned in the formation of basic trust is not just the correlation of routine, integrity, and reward. What is also mastered is an extremely sophisticated methodology of practical consciousness, which is a continuing protective device (although fraught with possibilities of fracture and disjunction) against the anxieties which even the most casual encounter with others can potentially provoke. (Giddens, 1990: 99)

The contradiction here between the activity required of us as participants in society constantly to engage with the challenges that life affords, and the passive acceptance of the structures of the taken-for-granted world which, precisely because they are taken-for-granted, would suggest that we do not need to engage consciously with them, is more apparent than real. Both are required. Both together are preconditions for effectiveness and sanity, for security and trust.

I have in an earlier study (Silverstone, 1994) discussed the role of the media in this project of building and sustaining trust. There I argued for the significant role television in particular, but radio before it, has had in enabling our ontological security, our trust in our institutions and our trust in the continuities of our everyday lives. The broadcast media emerged with the great expansions of suburbia in the inter-war period. Their role was enhanced during the Second World War, and, in a kind of repetition, the forties and the fifties saw television, the supremely suburban medium in anglophone societies especially, becoming deeply ingrained in what we all take for granted as an essential component of experienced reality.

We have come to depend on the media for this security. We trust them to be there always, and we panic when they break down. We rely on them for information about the world to which we would not have access without them, and we are reassured by the iterative familiarities of news and soap opera: characters we know, news readers whose voices and faces we recognize, structures of programming that we understand, can predict and essentially take for granted. Television is always on. The media are always with us. Both as background and as foreground. The continuities, the droning, of the music channel on the one hand; the management of crisis on the other. Despite the increasing cynicism of populations too sophisticated to take everything they read and hear as gospel, in times of trouble, national trouble, global trouble, trouble next door, we turn the radio on, we buy more newspapers, we watch more television news. Wall-to-wall news, even in the fragmenting world of cable and satellite, can be seen as an attempt to preserve this role: eternal television, never out of reach, always there.

Wall-to-wall news inoculates us from dread, from the numbing anxieties of a high-risk world. The media's capacity to engender trust is, of course, like so much else, double-edged. They invite denial as much as they encourage engagement. We can trust in the distance that they offer between us and the risks and challenges of the world, as well as trust their encouragement towards involvement. They occupy the space once held by superstition and religion, enabling us to frame our sense of ourselves reflexively against what we see and hear in relation to the world which exists somewhere on the other side of the screen or the loud-speaker, somewhere in cyberspace: heaven or hell.

The media are abstract systems in which we trust, which reinforce our willingness to trust other abstract systems, and which provide a structure for us to trust each other. Whether this trust is psychologically unsatisfying, as Anthony Giddens (1990: 113) argues, is a moot point. It depends on what is being measured against it, and what other sources of trust, including the personal, might be, or once were, available. And, indeed, such abstraction is neither uniform nor consistent. We live in a world in which mediated and non-mediated experiences intertwine. In the as-ifs of our relationships to public figures in their media representations, in our capacities to occupy the ersatz public spaces that the media from time to time offer us, and in what we take from the public articulations of morality and myth into our own private lives, the media are not simply or only abstract. Nor do they function without our active participation.

More problematic is the level of abstraction on which this argument depends. For in the world in which many of us live such trust is not always easy to come by, and trust itself is always dependent on the vicissitudes of history and circumstance. It can be disturbed and undermined as well as sustained. And, furthermore, trust, in its creation and its absence, is not innocent. It cannot be willed, but it can be created, or at least the conditions for its creation can be created. And in such activities, activities in which organizations as well as individuals are crucially involved, trust has become central to the operation of complex societies, in the pursuit of culture, the exercise of power and in the creation of the market. Trust, in modern and in post- or late-modern societies, has become a commodity.

Lynne Zucker, in a fascinating study, has examined the production of trust in the context of the emergence of a new economic and industrial order in the US in the 80 years between 1840 and 1920. In arguments which have their echo in those of E.P. Thompson (1971), where he discusses the breaking down of the moral economy of the pre-industrial world by the forces of the capitalist market, Zucker traces those factors which undermined confidence and trust in the early US market-place and in the relations between employers and their employees. She defines trust as a set of expectations shared by all involved in an exchange. Such expectations, she argues, are grounded in a sharing of basic norms of social behaviour and custom. And as such they are disrupted when the social norms are undermined or impossible to sustain. As societies in general become more complex, and the traditional forms of trust production, such as agreed procedures for exchange in traditional societies or the local or regional definitions of what counts as a social market in pre-industrial societies, come under pressure, then the importance of the institutionalized production of trust increases: 'If trust-producing mechanisms become institutionalised, and thus more formal, then trust becomes a saleable product, and the size of the market for trust determines the amount of trust produced' (Zucker, 1986: 54). Following just such disruption, the capacity of the US market to revive, indeed its capacity to function at all, depended on its ability to produce trust. Zucker traces both the logic and the institutional processes which secured the market for capital.

I would like, in what follows, briefly to trace her argument, and I do so for a number of reasons. The first is to illuminate the institutional responses to the nineteenth-century crisis of confidence in the basic conditions underpinning an effective market-place, conditions which, though not perhaps quite so dramatically, can be seen to be being revived in the new global and electronic twenty-first century market-place. The second is to develop a context for a discussion of the media's role in such a process, bearing in mind that the media are involved in two ways: as both institutions to deliver trust to the societies in which they are received, and at the same time as processes which need themselves to be trusted. And thirdly, and consequently, to suggest that the production of trust, in all its aspects, cannot be divorced from the media and, vice versa, that any study of the media must at some point or another confront its role in the creation of such trust.

Zucker distinguishes between background expectations of trust, the ones I have discussed already in the context of ontological security, and which require a common taken-for-granted universe and the reciprocity of perspectives, and constitutive expectations of trust, the rules that define a specific situation in which legitimate action is defined more or less precisely but in accordance with agreed sets of sometimes quite formalized expectations which all participants are expected to know and understand.

She then analyses three modes of trust production: process-based trust, which is dependent on continuities of culture and understanding, such as reputation or gift-exchange; characteristic-based trust, which is tied to the particular character and identity of persons, such as family or ethnicity; and institutionally-based trust which, as the term suggests, involves institutions, professions or intermediaries creating the conditions for the production and guarantee of trust. Whereas the first two modes of trust production, the process and the characteristic, do not generate a market in trust, the third does. The institutions that emerged within capitalism to create and protect the market, and to establish the conditions for its effective functioning, also created a market in trust: trust became then, and remains, a commodity.

The profound social changes which accompanied the industrialization of US society in the nineteenth century, and especially the scale of immigration and internal migration, created a set of conditions within which traditional forms of trust, those based on shared culture and memory, as well as those grounded in the authority of the person or the primary group, disintegrated, and as a result the economy faltered. The labour force was heterogeneous, and as a result trust between workers and employers was undermined. Process- and characteristic-based trust was confined only to homogeneous groups, among ethnic or geographically based minorities. They did not disappear and, of course, such bases for trust survive both in economic and certainly in social contexts. But they were unable to sustain the increasingly complex and diversifying economy. This could not survive without alternative sources of trust.

Zucker's argument is that trust could only be produced by a range of new institutions whose task it was to create the conditions for effective transactions across group boundaries, across geographical distance, and to enable the successful completion of an increasing number of interrelated, non-separable transactions. The institutions that emerged, the spread of rational bureaucratic organizations, professional credentialing, the service economy, including financial intermediaries and government, and regulation and legislation, perhaps above all the rise of insurance, together underpinned the market by creating the trust that enabled transactions to be undertaken safely and securely.

Trust is like information. It is not exhausted by use; the more there is, the more there is likely to be. Indeed, it is depleted by not being used (Gambetta, 1988: 234). The media in the modern world deliver both. But in times of change their capacity to do so effectively is undermined. As media change, the familiar certainties of our relationship to them can no longer be sustained. And as media change and claim new kinds of interaction and new kinds of sociability, the familiar forms of our relationship to each other, and to other institutions also, can no longer be guaranteed.

The new media invite us to trust them. They invite us to believe in the authenticity and authority of the electronic image and the electronic text. They invite us to believe in their truthfulness, honesty and security. They invite us to trust them with our money and our identities. They invite us to believe what we see and hear and to accept what they tell us, as more or less passive receivers of their communication or as actively using them to pursue our own agendas.

The expectation that we should engage in electronic commerce on the Internet requires us to make a double move: from the face-to-face on the one hand, and from familiar and taken-for-granted forms of mediation on the other. How can I trust the other through these disturbances and displacements? How can my continuing and willing participation in the complex affairs of society, especially in its economic and political life, be sustained? In the face of such uncertainty, how can my instinctive desire to withdraw, to privatize my behaviour, to regress to the primary group, to put my money under the mattress, my security in the hands of a vigilante and my citizenship in the cupboard, be stopped?

The commodification of trust. We see it all the time. We see it in the packaging of presidents and prime ministers and in the spinning of political webs. If you don't trust the messenger, the delivery system, then at least trust the symbol. Joe McGinniss' classic study of the Nixon presidential campaign was called *The Selling of a President* (1970), an acknowledgement of the necessary and patient work of constructing him as a trustworthy figure, despite his five o'clock shadow. Political appeals now depend on the claimed trustworthiness of the principal participants, a claim that displaces institutional trust in favour of trust based on characteristics. We call it 'presidentialism' and it is often blamed on the media, and on their role as both the seducer of, and the seduced within, the political process. It signals, ironically, the actual failure of trust in the abstract, political system. Maybe, on the other hand, it signals a continuing and persistent need to trust in the person. It is a wonder, however, that it still seems to work.

The same kind of regression in the market-place might seem to signal disaster. Yet that too is happening. Here too institutionally-based trust is being displaced by that based on characteristics, as if we really did live in a global village, a global market-place. The basic elements of trust in commerce, remembering that the term 'commerce' can be used to describe social as well as economic interaction – reciprocity and consistency – are being repackaged. Follow the brand. Trust is being signalled and claimed in the logo and the trade mark. That is what is being marketed. We have served you well so trust us, even in the new dealing environments. In the shift from off-line to on-line commerce *the brand is the transitional object*. It is the focus of a great deal of emotional and cognitive activity. It offers us security in a troubled world. It enables us to consume.

I would like to end this discussion with a number of questions. None of them is easy of answer, but each is fundamental for an understanding of the media in contemporary society and, in particular, for an understanding of media's role in underpinning and informing experience, in enabling us both to make sense of, and to manage, the world which now confronts us. They are questions that require us to study the media.

It is easier to mistrust than to trust. While it is never difficult to find evidence of untrustworthiness, it is virtually impossible to prove its positive mirror image (Luhmann, 1979, cited in Gambetta, 1988: 233). Under such conditions, then, how do we trust the media, both old and new, to be truthful, honest, secure? How do we know that the media trust us? How far do we need the media as a precondition for our capacity to trust each other? What happens to us and our society when these relations of trust are seen to break down? Can we rely on the media, as we increasingly appear to have to do, to make good the loss of institutional trust generated by and through the media? What institutions are now needed to ensure that trustworthy social, political and economic relations are generated and protected in our new electronic environment?

I will return to these questions in the last chapter of this book.

14 Memory

We appear to be living increasingly without history. The past, like the present, is fractured by division and indifference. The late-modern world re-invents itself nightly through costume drama and false memory. Traditions come late and languid. Remembrance is a dead end. We have lost the art of memory. Yet we are what we remember, as nations and as individuals; and memory is the site, now, of struggles for identity and for the ownership of a past. And these are bitter struggles that centre on memorials, monuments and museums. Bitter struggles for the past not to be forgotten; for the past to be claimed for the present and the present to be claimed for the future. But what past, and whose?

With the decline of oral culture we no longer need, ourselves, collectively to remember. We have records and texts for that – *aides-mémoire*, *médias de memoire* – that displace memory away from the inner workings of minds. Oral memory was both a technique and a resource. The one fixed it for persuasion and control; the other enabled it to grow through the generations, sustained by public ritual and private tales. Stories not fragments. Beliefs not fantasies. References not representations.

With the rise of writing and science, both collective and personal memory became an object: to be fixed and investigated, challenged and analysed. History and psychoanalysis are both sciences of the past, though often at odds. Memory in both becomes something of a plaything. Plastic and clay. Indeed history is supposed to erase memory, to make it redundant through the certainties of fixed narratives, documentary sources and the tyranny of facts. Abstraction rather than recollection. And psychoanalysis is supposed to investigate memory, to enquire into its power and into its disturbance. Memory is energy, both creative and destructive of individuality, of the self.

For both history and psychoanalysis memory is at best, therefore, a resource; and neither history nor psychoanalysis offers any certainties. The authority of both is subject to challenge. Indeed the authority of each is challenged by the authority of the other. History challenges psychoanalysis in the matter of false memory syndrome, and psychoanalysis challenges history as a singular, literal tale. Memory, as a consequence, resumes its significance, and its relationship to history, as indeed its relationship to mind, is unstable and shifting. Memory, as Raphael Samuel argues:

> so far from being merely a passive receptacle or storage system, an image bank of the past, is rather an active, shaping force; that it is dynamic – what it contrives symptomatically to forget is as important as what it remembers – and that it is dialectically related to historical thought, rather than being some kind of negative other to it. What Aristotle called anamnesis, the conscious act of recollection, was an intellectual labour very much akin to that of the historian: a matter of quotation, imitation, borrowing and assimilation. After its own fashion it was a way of constructing knowledge. (Samuel, 1994: x)

Memory, for Samuel, is what is done in recollection, with or without tranquillity, through oral testimony and shareable discourse. It is where the private threads of the past are woven into public cloth, offering an alternative vision, an alternative reality to the official accounts of the academy and the archive. These memories inaugurate other texts, no less historical than the first, but nevertheless other. They emerge from the popular and the personal and they are the product of their own times. In the fluidity of such memories the past emerges as a complex rather than a singular reality, and, as others have argued, the plurality of memory is itself evidence of the plurality of reality, and not in some sense, necessarily, a mistake. Memories shift in the remembrance and in the telling. Memories are disputed and contested, though there is always a claim somewhere that there is reality outside memory to act as judge and jury. But we know, do we not, that historical facts are only of significance in so far as they are of significance, and that significance is a matter of value, not truth (though truth, of course, is a value).

We cannot ignore memory, even if we no longer know quite what to do with it. Memory, like so much, is now a problem not a solution. And memory in the conjunction of the private and the public is not just personal. It is, indeed, and without qualification, political.

This is my topic in this chapter. In it I want to suggest the centrality of memory for experience, both the experience of the individual and the experience of cultures. I want to suggest that memory is what we have, in private and public, to fix ourselves in space and especially in time. And I want to suggest that our media, both by intention and default, are instruments for the articulation of memory. Memory which is public, popular, pervasive, plausible and, therefore, both compelling and from time to time also compulsive. What are the implications of the contemporary media's playfulness with the past? As storyteller, as archive, as the provider of the souvenir? And how are we to understand the media's power in defining the terms as well as the content of such memory and memories?

My own past, no less than that of the nation, is bound up with the images and the sounds of a mediated past. My nostalgia for another age, my other age, is constructed through memories of programmes and advertisements watched or listened to in childhood. These are the raw materials, in part, for sharing that past with others. A mutual claiming of identities of class and culture. And I can remember media images of great events, assassinations, coronations, four-minute miles, just as the media themselves now have their own past to remember.

But above all, in the absence of other sources, the media have the power to define the past: to present and represent it. They claim historical authority in drama and documentary: versions of realism that have no referent other than in other tales and other images. The mobilization of witnesses; the reconstruction of situations and encounters; the uncovering of evidence: the rhetoric of truth. Here as elsewhere, this is the claim. To remember. To define the past. This is how it was. Imagine.

Classical, Renaissance and Romantic memory depended on images. Images to represent its structure and images to represent its content. Early rhetoricians and magicians built mental models of the architecture of public spaces, theatres and the heavens as structures within which memory was constructed and prodigious features of applied memory were thereby enabled. Simonides, Thomas Aquinas and Giordano Bruno built the elaborate mnemonics ('mnemotechnics' as they are described by Frances Yates, 1964, 1966) to fix the past and the otherwise unrecoverable in mind. Indeed, as Frances Yates documents so brilliantly, the art of memory became an art of magic in the hands of the occult masters of the Renaissance; an early example, perhaps, of the potent combination of image, technology, metaphor and belief which then and now underpins the capacity to construct public memory and represent it. Such was their power to command attention; such was their power to define the past and through the past therefore to claim the future.

But throughout the medieval world images of the past were everywhere. The world was to be read in its visibility. The meanings inscribed in stained-glass windows and in the sacred geographies of shrines were there for the taking. The rhetoric of those images called on familiar symbolisms of culture and belief and at the same time were open enough to engage the private thoughts of the believer, to prompt, perhaps, an intersection of public and private memories. And so it remains.

Memory is effective. The texts that claim it for us in public space, be they single images, films or memorials, are significant because through them an otherwise inaccessible reality is constructed. And it is that reality which commands attention, claims belief and initiates action. In this sense 'life' and 'life in-writing', in James E. Young's words, are necessarily and fundamentally interrelated. Writing about the Holocaust, he refuses the separation of history and narration, as well as the innocence of the unmediated event. 'Literature remembers past destructions even as it shapes our practical responses to current crisis' (Young, 1990: 4). And not just literature, and not just the cultural products of the elite, of course.

It is from these debates that my claims for the centrality of media as keystones for the construction of contemporary memory emerge. There is no unambiguous divide between the historical and the popular representation of the past. They fuse together, as well as compete, in public space. And together they define for us both texts and contexts: for identity, for community and, perhaps most significant of all and underlying both, for belief and action. To study the media's relationship to memory is not to deny the authority of the event which is the focus of recollection, but it is to insist on the media's capacity to construct a public past, as well as a past for the public. The texture of memory is intertwined with the texture of experience. Memory is work: it is never shaped in a vacuum, nor are its motives ever pure (Young, 1993: 2). Memory is struggle. And therefore it is wise to struggle over memory.

Consider the Holocaust.

But how to begin? With an acknowledgement perhaps that at this time, at this time of writing, the time in which those who survived are surviving no longer, in which the possibility of testimony is dribbling away in the sands of time, this human tragedy has at last to be fixed in time. That this is the time when it becomes possible for a new generation, the sons and the daughters, to claim their ownership of what can now only be the referred pain of history; a time when the Western world is obsessed with what it cannot any longer know, but somehow, and rightly, desires not to forget; a time for memorial and monument; a time when it seems that the time has come for the casting of the sounds and stones of memory, fixing the past, fixing it for all to see, fixing it for all time.

But how does one remember such terrible wounds? For years there has been silence. Everything not said. The cracks of history well and truly papered over. Yet now we find ourselves remembering: forcing memory out of witnesses and out of records. Historians and the media, both. Writing and rewriting and writing again. The survivors and the children of the survivors, for only survivors can see. To remember, to record and to try to understand.

We seem now compelled to fill the recent emptiness with sights and sites, sounds and words and pictures. To ignore Adorno's proscription against poetry. To ignore the commandment forbidding the graven image. To turn the negative into the positive. To believe that time cannot erode the meaning of memory. Of course the media cannot be silent. And we must not be allowed to forget. But what should we remember and who has the rights of narration and inscription?

In the city of Kassel there is a monument to the Holocaust which can no longer be seen. It is sunk beneath the earth. The monument, designed by Horst Hoheisel, was built to replace a fountain funded by a Jewish entrepreneur and built in the city in 1908. It was destroyed by the Nazis as 'a Jewish fountain' in 1939, two years before the first transport containing the city's Jews left the railway station for Riga and then onwards. Hoheisel designed a negative monument. Whereas before there was a fountain, there is now a well; and what was before a pyramid rising 12 metres into the air, is now buried under the square. 'The sunken fountain is not the memorial at all. . . . It is only history turned into a pedestal, an invitation to passers-by who stand upon it to search for the memorial in their own heads. For only there is the memorial to be found' (Hoheisel, quoted in Young, 1993: 46). It is those who visit and stand in the empty space who become, both by default and intention, the monument and the memorial. James E. Young, to whom I am indebted for this account, summarizes what he sees as the significance of this:

> The counter-monument . . . forces the memorial to disperse – not gather – memory, even as it gathers the literal effects of time in one place. In dissipating itself over time, the counter-monument would mimic time's own dispersion, become more like time than memory. It would remind us that the very notion of linear time assumes memory of a past moment: time as the perpetually measured distance between this moment and the next, between this instant and a past remembered. In this sense, the counter-monument asks us to recognise that time and memory are interdependent, in dialectical flux. (Young, 1993: 46–7)

Our media, for the most part, refuse this option, this possibility, this reticence. And in so doing, whatever else they do, they fuse memory to a particular time. It is said that, once monumentally enshrined in memorials or museums, the life of memory disappears; that monuments in whatever form can be seen as substitutes for memory, as displacements or denials. And this must also be true for our media's representations of the past. Or at least we need to bear it in mind.

So when we enquire into what is now produced as a call for the past, for memory, and in particular for the recall of the Holocaust in popular culture and contemporary media, we should not forget that what we now create as memory is also historically and socially situated. Our accounts emerge from our own concerns, the preoccupations of the here and now. They cannot be divorced from the conditions of their production: as moments of mediation in the complex and commodified spaces of popular culture and everyday life.

Steven Spielberg's film, *Schindler's List* (1993), has therefore to be seen through the number of veils that separate it from its object. Time first of all. But then also a primary narrative in Thomas Kinneally's book, a book which already begins the distillation of a large-scale and unimaginable horror into the life of a single man and a thousand or so survivors. The Holocaust involved mass destruction, and not just of Jews. Both Kinneally and Spielberg tell a tale of particular survival. And of course through the particular but, because this is now film, also the general. The final sequence of the film in which survivors of the event, as well as the actors who played them in the film, emerge over a grassy knoll as if for all the world they were extras in *The Sound of Music*, draws the viewer into a narrative of hope, of sentiment and immortality. It draws this tale away from the horror of its images of the unknown and indeed unknowable to the comfort of the familiar.

This is Hollywood at work. Hollywood 'bearing witness'. Spielberg 'telling the truth' (both cited in David Ansen, 'Spielberg's Obsession', *Newsweek*, 20 December 1993: 114, 112, quoted in Zelizer, 1997). And what Hollywood does with memory is to contain it. It draws its sting. Much has been made, in relation to this film and to Spielberg's later *Saving Private Ryan* (1998), of the honesty and truthfulness of the images. The destruction of the Cracow ghetto, the sequence in the gas chambers, the landings on the Normandy beaches, claim a veracity that is shocking. This is as close, as real, as it gets. The survivors have testified to it. And they have, of course, their own memories. For the rest of us, hypnotized by scenes of horror, what we remember is the film. We have been offered, and may well accept, screen memories, screened memories: the subjunctive but also the definitive. We have nowhere else to go in time. The Holocaust becomes the movie. The movie becomes the Holocaust.

There are many issues here, of course. Too many for these pages. Spielberg's representational strategy is in drama, in narrative and in the power of the reconstructed image. Not for him the dust of testimony, of the witness struggling with his or her own tale. There is power in both of course. Whereas the former leaves little to the imagination, the latter requires attention to the word. And the word offers, it does not compel, an image. Claude Lanzmann's nine-hour documentary *Shoah* (1985) is well known for taking the latter route. Direct representation for him is anathema. The Holocaust 'is above all unique in that it erects a ring of fire around itself. . . . Fiction is a transgression. I deeply believe that there are some things that cannot and should not be represented' (Lanzmann, 1994, cited in Hartmann, 1997: 63).

Shoah avoids the possible dangers of the desensitizing effects of direct images of violence by representing nothing but memories of it. Lanzmann has taken the route suggested by the Hoheisal sculpture, and *Shoah* in the same way is a counter-monument to the Holocaust. Indeed Spielberg, too, has initiated a major project of video recordings of private testimony. Is there more power, more honesty, in the witness's tale or in the story-teller's? In fact or in fiction? There are too many paradoxes here to unravel.

Either way what we have to confront is the mediation of memory: fragments of the past translated through time, and projected as on the cinema screen, into the future. Media memories are mediated memories. Technology has both connected and intervened. We have been offered supplements to experience: *vitamins of time*.

Geoffrey Hartmann, in a brilliant discussion of some of these themes, specifically in relation to the filmic representation of the Holocaust, makes a wider point, one which will allow me too to move back from the specific to the general and from the texture of memory to the texture of experience. He is addressing the double life of the mimetic image, its comfort but also its disturbance:

> In a society of the spectacle, strong images are what property or the soil is often said to be: a need of the soul. If the incidence of recovered memory seems to have increased dramatically in recent years, it may be that images of violence relayed hourly by the media, as well as widespread publicity of the Holocaust that leads to metaphorical appropriations (Sylvia Plath is a famous case), have popularised the idea of a determining trauma. It is understandable that many might feel a pressure to find within themselves, and for public show, an experience equally decisive and bonding, a sublime or terrible identity mark. (Hartmann, 1997: 72–3)

We are back to the conjunction of history and psychoanalysis, of the political and the personal, and of the play of mediation. We are also back in the realm of performance. Hartmann is suggesting that our media's preoccupation with the past, and with the past as trauma, is ripe for the picking. The once buried and now dramatically displayed images are part of the currency of daily life. We all have, or seem to need, our own private holocaust to claim and to justify present pain. Indeed these images, and the process of their construction, in witnessing, are there for us as models and metaphors. To make them our own. This is most unexpected. Yet it is understandable. For the display of memory is also an invitation: to compare, to adopt, to appropriate. The experiences of others are harmonized to each other and to our own in the continuities of their mediation and reproduction, and the lines between the public and private, self and other, present and past, truth and falsehood are, as a result, neither singular nor clear.

These media memories are there for the taking and for the fighting over. All memory is partial. And in the rhetoric of the media what is being offered is a particular vision of a past which includes as well as excludes. That is why the battles over memory are fought so vehemently; why others claim different pasts and refuse the limits of one interpretation of events. History is the anvil on which identities are forged; memory is the site of so many claims and counter-claims: for nationhood, for personhood. And it is popular history, popular memory, which is increasingly at stake: the unofficial knowledge over which the media lord.

The media offer us their versions of the past, which are, of course, versions of our pasts made visible. Not all of these images have the power, the resonance or indeed the discomfort of the Holocaust. On the contrary. Televised adaptations of Jane Austen's novels or dramatic representations of life below stairs, as well as documentary accounts of the secret lives of famous figures, offer a continuous diet of times past as pastimes. They enable as well as constrain the imagination. They give dignity as well as strip it away. As Raphael Samuel argues (1994: 235), in an eloquent defence of the heritage industry, the BBC had a crucial role to play in sensitizing a nation to its past, and in particular the folk past, the past of the folk.

I began this chapter by referring to the common perception of our postmodern age: that it is without history. Maybe this is not quite right. Rather than an absence of history, it might be suggested that there is now too much of it. The grand narratives have not been lost, just reconstructed. And they are being reconstructed on a daily basis on our media screens. All our narratives are grand. All claim attention. All are subject to constant interrogation and analysis.

Theodor Adorno (1954), quoting Leo Lowenthal, once described television as psychoanalysis in reverse, suggesting, or so it seems to me, the medium's capacity to construct rather than deconstruct the layers of the unconscious, and to reproduce seductively in its programmes the masking and mirroring of the mind. My argument suggests that the media – film, television and radio above all – could be described equally well (or badly) as history in reverse. They produce texts for the popular imagination, equally layered and equally suggestive. Memory is what unites the two. Memory as the product of media, and not only its precondition. Memory as a claim for us to identify with a common as well as a singular past. My own claim, of course, is that there is no separation to be had between mediated and non-mediated memory. And, consequently, if we are to try to understand the ways in which biography and history are intertwined, then we have to take this interpenetration into account. We have, necessarily, to study the media's public rhetoric of memory.

15 The Other

> [T]he Other is in no way another myself, participating with me in a common existence. The relationship with the Other is not an idyllic and harmonious relationship of communion or a sympathy through which we put ourselves in the Other's place; we recognise the Other as resembling us, but as exterior to us; the relationship with the Other is a relationship with a Mystery.
>
> Emmanuel Levinas, *Time and the Other*

This chapter is about others, otherness, the Other. Capital O. The O signifies. It refers to the recognition that there is something out there that is not me, not of my making, not under my control; distinct, different, beyond reach, yet occupying the same space, the same social landscape. The Other includes others: people I know or have never heard of; my friends as well as my enemies. It includes my neighbours as well as those I have only seen in photographs and on screens. It includes those in the past as well as those in the future. In my society and in yours. But because I and the Other share a world, because I will be your Other as much you are mine, even if I know you not, then I have a relationship to you. That relationship is a challenge. Through it I am forced to recognize that I am not alone, that I have, in one way or another, to take the Other into account.

In so doing, what am I and what am I doing? The short answer is that I become a moral being and that, in principle at least, I act, or can act, ethically. In having to take the Other into account I am, as Colin Davis suggests 'confronted with real choices between responsibility and obligation towards the Other, or hatred and violent repudiation. The Other invests me with genuine freedom, and will be the beneficiary or victim of how I decide to exercise it' (Davis, 1996: 48–9). Without the Other, I am lost.

Experience, therefore, has other people in it. And life among them is, by definition, a moral life, even in its occasional or chronic immorality. In this chapter I want to consider this fundamental dimension of experience, the ground base of social life, and enquire into the media's relationship to it. Such an enquiry will not be particularly easy, not least because of the discomfort these days in pursuing a moral discourse. In these relativist times, the moral itself is perceived as other – beyond the pale and dangerous. Sociologists, as Zygmunt Baumann (1989) has argued, have shied away from such discussions, finding in the social the origins of morality, but not making, let alone rushing, to judgement. If societies are the fount of moral life, then each society will have its own morality, and who are we to judge the ethical codes of our neighbours? Such relativism, even if we believe it inescapable, even if we argue for its necessity (for absolutism in moral matters, we know, will lead to tyranny) is however troubling. There are enough moments in history and in the present when both individuals and societies are forced to confront what is judged to be the immorality of others, as well as our own: but how to make those judgements and how to make them consistently?

All of what we do, all of who we are, as subjects and actors in the social world, depends on our relationships to others: how we see them, know them, relate to them, care for or ignore them. Seeing them is crucial. Anthropologists have long noted how the study of other societies and cultures illuminates our own, just as they have struggled with the problems of representing the Other in texts and tales that somehow must pass the muster of translation from one culture to another. How do I represent the Other in what I write or film without, on the one hand, exoticizing him or her? How do I represent the Other in what I write or film without, on the other hand, absorbing him or her into my own sense of myself?

The Other, however, can act as a mirror, and in the recognition of difference we construct our own identity, our own sense of ourselves, in the world. If we understand these differences, or even if we merely see them, then we have to take the Other into account. We can neither presume that the world is simply as we know it, that it is merely a projection of our experience; nor can we erase it, pretend that it does not exist. We have to acknowledge, indeed, that there are things that we do not, cannot, fully understand. That the world is mysterious, enigmatic.

Emmanuel Levinas, one of the most difficult of twentieth-century philosophers, who I have already cited at the beginning of this chapter, constructs an argument and a view of the world with the moral at its core. But in doing so he does not offer a specific version of the moral life; not a code, an ethical *code*. His philosophy dwells on morality, the ethical, as a precondition for social life, and not its consequence. The argument insists that it is my being with others that is the fundamental existential fact. And in being with others I have to take responsibility for others. I have to take such responsibility without any expectation that others will take responsibility for me. Responsibility without reciprocity. It is an awesome thought. But Levinas proposes it as the primary structure of subjectivity. Morality is asymmetrical. In this he is at one with Dostoyevsky, who writes in *The Brothers Karamazov*, 'We are all responsible for all and for all men before all, and I more than all the others' and with Deuteronomy (24: 17–22), in its insistence on care for the alien, the orphan and the widow.

Responsibility in turns requires a duty of care, and I can only care for those who are close to me. Responsibility requires proximity, though not necessarily physical proximity. Correlatively, distance spells danger. And society is no longer seen as the necessary guarantee of moral order, but as a resource for society to exploit or expel it. In Baumann's words:

> Morality is not a product of society. Morality is something society manipulates – exploits, re-directs, jams. Obversely, immoral behaviour, a conduct which forsakes or abdicates responsibility for the other, is not an effect of social malfunctioning. It is therefore the incidence of immoral, rather than moral, behaviour which calls for the investigation of the social administration of subjectivity. (Baumann, 1989: 183)

I have chosen to begin my discussion of otherness with Levinas, and with his interpreters Colin Davis and Zygmunt Baumann, because I believe it provides an elegant, and in most respects convincing, approach to morality grounded, as it is, in an enquiry into the status of the Other. In this it is provocative. In this it is, itself, moral.

But his work is relevant for another reason, one implied by Anthony Giddens (1991) in his consideration of the distinctiveness of what he calls late modernity as compared to the pre-modern and the modern. 'Taken overall', he writes (Giddens, 1991: 27), 'the many diverse modes of culture and consciousness characteristic of pre-modern "world systems" formed a genuinely fragmented array of human social communities. By contrast, late modernity produces a situation in which humankind in some respects becomes a "we", facing problems and opportunities where there are no "others".' Globalization creates a single world; unification goes hand in hand with fragmentation. But what happens to us when 'there are no "others" '? What happens to us when we do not see the other either because they seem the same as us, or so far removed from us that they have no status, no meaning for us?

There are two problems here. Both involve, as I shall argue, the media. Both require, and this of course is my point, that we take the media into account in confronting them. The first has to do with distance. The second with subjectivity.

Let me start with distance. Baumann is unequivocal. His analysis of the Holocaust, and his explanation of its possibility, are grounded in his understanding of the capacity of German society to expel its Jews from its imagination before expelling them from life. Central to this project was the creation of institutional and technological processes, the product of the rational and efficient mind, which dealt with the Jews as a problem, and for which extermination was the solution. Society repressed morality by the creation of distance. The Jews were no longer human. They were *other*, not the Other in Levinas's sense, but the other as beyond care and beyond responsibility. The Jews had to be pushed beyond otherness. This was distance and distancing at work.

We are encouraged to believe that the new media will change all this. A book on the new communications revolution is called *The Death of Distance* (Cairncross, 1997). It argues for the benefits of the new scale of human life enabled by digitalization and electronic networks. It lists 30 ways in which our lives will be transformed, mostly economically, less certainly politically, but also socially. It sees in the increasing intensity of global communication a greater understanding and greater tolerance of human beings in other parts of the globe.

But distance cannot be erased by technology. A telephone call will keep people apart even as it connects them. Connection is not the problem. It does not guarantee proximity. We are still confronted with the problem of distance. New media technologies do not stop war or genocide. They can make them more efficient (information in the service of destruction) as well as invisible (information in the service of dissemblance). They can keep us apart by providing images which disable care and responsibility: images of conflicts without bloodshed, bombing without damage, battles without armies, war without victims. Actions without consequence. In this, Jean Baudrillard (1995) was right when he argued that the Gulf War did not take place. Television intervened. It did not connect. Technology can isolate and annihilate the Other. And without the Other we are lost.

And technology can annihilate distance in the opposite way. It can bring the Other too close, too close for us to recognize difference and distinctiveness. Foreign policies are conducted on the basis that the world is merely a projection of ourselves. The interweaving of global images; the appropriation of the cultures to our own agendas (how often now is the 'primitive' in the shape of dancing Africans or the impoverished slum dweller a feature in global advertising?); the expectation that given half a chance the world would like to become just like us. Of course the Russians understand democracy. And even documentary images of other worlds have to conform to our own preconceptions. The poor must look poor; the starving must have swollen bellies and flies in their eyes. Technologically induced familiarity may not breed contempt, but it arguably breeds indifference. If things are too close we do not see them. In this too technology can isolate and annihilate the Other. And without the Other we are lost.

Media representations, the communications we undertake that transcend the limits of the face-to-face, those that breach propinquity, have consequences for how we see and live in the world. They frame as well as inform experience. They require an ethical response but do not, on the face of it, provide us with much in the way of resources for that ethical response. The technologies that enable and sustain late modern societies in all their complexity, and supremely among them our media technologies, seem to have changed the ethical universe, which traditionally at least was contained in time and space and which, traditionally at least, enabled us to follow through the consequences of actions; confronting the world as it confronts us.

There is a sense here, hard though it is both to articulate and to acknowledge, that contrary to what is often argued – that in the global reach of modern media we confront the world in its Otherness as never before, and that in that confrontation we can be seen and shown to care (the rise of the environmental movement is a case in point) – the media are in a structural sense amoral. Amoral, not immoral. The distance they create and mask as closeness, the connections that they make, while keeping us apart, their vulnerability to dissemblance (from the faking of documentary images to the disguise of identity in Internet communication) reduces the visibility, the vividness, of the Other.

It follows that the 'as-if' of our media world is, in many ways, too, amoral. And this notwithstanding the many powerful programmes, media events or news reports that break through the defended sensibilities of everyday life. This is a shocking conclusion, more so because, as I have argued throughout this book, the media are so central to experience. And this amorality is expressed, perhaps even reinforced, by the essential ephemerality and substitutability of media and media representation. If we do not like one thing, we can turn to another. If we do not like one thing it will disappear soon anyway. Off the screens, slipping over the edge of the world, like an omelette out of its pan.

And this slippage is manifest too, as a result, in the devaluation and the disintegration of the moral self. As Zygmunt Baumann (1993: 198) observes:

> The moral self is the most evident and the most prominent among technology's victims. The moral self can not and does not survive fragmentation. In the world mapped by wants and pock-marked by hurdles to their speedy gratification, there is ample room left for *homo ludens*, *homo oeconomicus* and *homo sentimentalis*; for the gambler, entrepreneur, or hedonist – but none for the moral subject. In the universe of technology, the moral self with

> its negligence of rational calculation, disdain of practical uses and indifference to pleasure feels and is an unwelcome alien.

This view of the world fits well with many analyses of the high modern or post-modern condition, above all in its stress on fragmentation. Baumann is talking about the fragmentation of the subject. Anthony Giddens, in his suggestive analysis of what he calls the 'sequestration of experience' also pursues this perception by identifying the ways in which portions of the world which once upon a time confronted us, as dilemmas or horrors, but as an integrated part of life to be led, have to a significant degree been placed outside direct experience by institutions designed to reduce the challenges of, and to, the everyday. Madness, criminality, sickness and death, sexuality and nature, all have been placed beyond sight and touch by institutions created to reduce uncertainty and anxiety (Giddens, 1991: 144–80). Society has, in Giddens's argument, separated us from life, and one of the unintended consequences of such a development has been the repression of 'a cluster of basic moral and existential components of human life that are, as it were, squeezed to the sidelines' (1991: 167). Giddens notes the significance of media to this process, without developing the argument, and without identifying media's centrality both to the process and to its legitimation.

Fragmentation, then, can be seen to affect both institutions and individuals. The moral subject is no more. Well, perhaps. Levinas's fundamental critique of Western philosophy, and in particular its development in the phenomenology of Husserl and Heidegger, on which his own work was based, was that it had crucially ignored the Other. What had emerged, in his view, was a philosophy that constructed the subject as a monad, historically and sociologically disconnected, perceptually omnipotent in seeking an understanding of the world only through the individual's capacity to apprehend it or construct it. Others have made the same point sociologically by identifying the narcissistic turn that Western culture at least has taken since the Enlightenment. The Cartesian elision of cogito and ego was, it appears, fatal. Individual subjects had no connection with each other. Both philosophical and social space was fragmented and islands we became.

Yet there is another version of this fragmentation in discussions of the high modern subject. Not the monad, but the nomad. Baumann suggests as much, though others have pursued it with more ferocity. Subjectivity and identity, far from being singular, are now conceived as plural: performed, played with, authentic only perhaps in their inauthenticity; structured in their lack of structure; consistent in their inconsistency. The differentiated subject moves through the world, chameleon-like, with stripes and spots forever a-changing. And this movement too is mediated, reflected in the media, refracted in the media, enabled by the media, and defined by our relationship to the media in their various manifestations. Marx's dream that in the new age he could 'hunt in the morning, fish in the afternoon, rear cattle in the evening, criticise after dinner, just as I have a mind, without ever becoming hunter, fisherman, shepherd or critic' (Marx and Engels, 1970: 53) has been rapidly overtaken by the so-called progress of modernity, where I can be male in the morning, female in the afternoon, and maybe something else entirely after dinner, and where my tastes, styles and person can change with each moment of consumption.

If morality lies in the relation between self and Other, then a degree of integrity is required for both. And that integrity must in turn be sought if not found in the consistencies of experience, and in what, without wishing to be portentous, I would call the struggle for the moral life.

I want to locate this struggle, and the media's centrality to it, in two places. In private and in public. In private, within the households of the world, public communications and values, mediated no doubt through speakers and screens, become subject to what I have in another context called the 'moral economy' of the household (Silverstone, 1994). I confess that in earlier discussions of the moral economy, I was uncomfortable with the notion of the moral. I was discussing morality with a very small and non-judgemental *m*. Here I want to suggest something stronger, but certainly more contentious: that the domestic is one significant place where the struggle for the moral life takes place in our society, and it is a struggle which involves the desire and capacity to position ourselves as sentient, caring beings in relation to the Other. It is a struggle because it does not always, or even ever fully, succeed.

However, it is the case that, once ideas, images, values and so-called truths cross the threshold between public and private lives and spaces, their meanings are subject to re-examination, rejection, transcendence, in accordance with a set of values that sustain, uniquely, the social group, the family or otherwise, that occupies that private space. It is indeed in relation to the media, to mediated communication and representation, that we increasingly have to position ourselves as moral subjects, for the Other appears to us often in no other guise, and those representations are checked, where possible, against the lived experiences of everyday life. In this way the essential amorality of media meets, still, the sites of resistance in cultures, indeed both public and private, that can call the media to account. In this way the piercing generalizations of high modern theory meet their own challenge: the ways of everyday life of those in the world.

The second dimension of the struggle for the moral life concerns the public appearance of truth. Truth in the media is like community in society: only discovered to be of value and becoming the focus of public concern when it is about to disappear. Two cases, at this time of writing, preoccupy the British media. The first concerns a British documentary film, *The Connection*, made in the UK by a major public broadcaster, transmitted globally and a winner of numerous awards, which has been revealed to have involved substantial faking in its claims to represent the reality of drug-smuggling from Colombia to the UK. The second, reported in the same newspaper, was the apparent falsehoods in the autobiography of Nobel peace prize-winner Rigoberto Menchú. In both cases the charge is that there is a reality against which to assess the accuracy and truthfulness of the narrated accounts. There appears to have been little public defence of the documentary film-maker who might have argued that what the film represented was what he knew to be true but had in some measure to create, and which in the interests of narrative tension in an age starved of 'unmediated reality' he claimed (untruthfully) was happening in real time. In the second case a defence has been proposed: and it lies in the right of a writer (for political or other reason) to use metaphor and rhetoric to dramatize an incompletely true story for effect and impact. In both cases a general truth can be seen to be being claimed beneath a literal falsehood. Memory, as we have seen, is often no more nor less.

We are right to be concerned, but we seem naïve, often, in our approach. We need better understanding of the implications of what is now happening to truth as a result, especially and increasingly, of technology's capacity to distance ourselves from it; as it were, in spades. The dead now appear (though the dead, once recorded, never really die) in new sequences on our screens, digitally remastered from existing images and formatted into new sequences: body and soul; sound and image, selling us perfumes, soft drinks and cars. The digital world is bound to lie. It takes the amorality of media to new heights.

What are we to do?

I will hazard some suggestions in my concluding chapter. For the moment I want to return to where I began. To the ground base of ethics in the acknowledgement of the Other. I propose that the study of the media must be ethical in this sense. Indeed, it cannot but be, for in examining the roots of representation and the ways in which the media provide access to the material and symbolic Other; in examining how the relationships between us and them and between each other are to be managed and judged; and in understanding these relationships as the source of struggle for a moral life, our studies of the media go to the heart of what we now must take to be the human condition.

It is fitting to end this chapter with a quotation from the philosopher whose work began the first, Isaiah Berlin. In introducing his own essay on the pursuit of the ideal, in a book vividly titled *The Crooked Timber of Humanity*, he has this to say on the subject of ethics:

> Ethical thought consists of the systematic examination of the relations of human beings to each other, the conceptions, interests and ideals from which human ways of treating one another spring, and the systems of value on which such ends of life are based. These beliefs about how life should be lived, what men and women should be and do, are objects of moral enquiry; and when applied to groups and nations, and, indeed mankind as a whole, are called political philosophy, which is but ethics applied to society. (Berlin, 1990: 1–2)

In so far as the relations between human beings now depend on their mediation electronically, and our treatment of each other, and each other's conceptions, interests and ideals, depends on their communication through the same media, and in so far as those media are recognized to have changed both the scale and the scope of such relations, then we have to accept the challenge. If we are to understand, once again in Berlin's words, the 'often violent world in which we live', and our media's role in that world, then we are *de facto* engaged in ethical enquiry.

16 Towards a new media politics

It is all about power, of course. In the end. The power the media have to set an agenda. The power they have to destroy one. The power they have to influence and change the political process. The power to enable, to inform. The power to deceive. The power to shift the balance of power: between state and citizen; between country and country; between producer and consumer. And the power that they are denied: by the state, by the market, by the resistant or resisting audience, citizen, consumer. It is all about ownership and control: the who and the what and the how of it. And it is about the drip, drip, drip of ideology as well as the shock of the luminous event. It is about the media's power to create and sustain meanings; to persuade, endorse and reinforce. The power to undermine and reassure. It is about reach. And it is about representation: the ability to present, reveal, explain; and also the ability to grant access and participation. It is about the power to listen and the power to speak and be heard. The power to prompt and guide reflection and reflexivity. The power to tell tales and articulate memories.

We study the media because we are concerned about their power: we fear it, we decry it, we adore it. The power of definition, of incitement, of enlightenment, of seduction, of judgement. We study the media because of the need to understand how powerful the media are in our everyday lives; in the structuring of experience; on the surface and in the depths. And we want to harness that power for good rather than ill.

The title of this chapter is deliberately ambiguous. It can be read in two ways. Is the issue to be a new kind of politics for the media, or a politics for the world of new media? The answer is, of course, both. Things are changing and the changing media are both cause and consequence of those changes. Whereas once we could think of the media's political role as one dominated more or less exclusively by the ideals of a free press and public service broadcasting, we can no longer do so. The fragmentation and fracturing of media space, the liberalization of media markets, as well as the digital destruction of the politics of spectrum scarcity; the opportunities enabled by the falling cost of entry to media, on the one hand, and the constraints posed by the rising costs of success in a global media culture, on the other; all are indications of a new kind of media space which will have profound implications for the exercise of power as well as the opportunities for public participation in political life. As broadcasters become publishers; as markets for goods become markets for images; as the centre of political gravity continues to shift from the dispatch box to the box in the corner; and as Larry Flynt, pornographer supreme, threatens to start dissecting the private lives of Senators and Congressmen on the pages of *The Hustler*, as his small contribution to the politics and public life of the United States, we are forced to recognize new political realities emerging with which the existing political process and existing political institutions will be hard pushed to deal.

Whereas once we might have thought of the media as an appendage to the political process, a handmaiden for governments and parties, as well as an irritant or a watchdog, the Fourth Estate, we now have to confront them as fundamentally inscribed into the political process itself. Politics, like experience, can no longer even be considered outside a media frame. Whereas once we might have thought of the media as a guarantor of liberty and of the democratic process, we now have to recognize how it has been that the very freedoms demanded by, and granted to, the media, and which have served us so well in the past, are on the verge of being destroyed by those very same media in their florid maturity. The media, no less than perhaps global capitalism as a whole, as John Gray (1998) in his sustained critique would argue, are biting from the hand that feeds: both media and market freedoms are on the verge of destroying themselves. We have turned cultural cannibal. This is a terrible paradox, but one that must be understood and confronted.

It is, however, extraordinary to note how often the media are distinguished by their marginalization, if not their complete absence, in so many of the critiques of the current state of global society (Beck, 1992; Giddens, 1998; Gray, 1998; Soros, 1998). How it is possible to discuss globalization, reflexivity and the management of risk without placing the media as central beats me. Global economies and global finance cannot work without a global information infrastructure, and are threatened by the same media technologies: speed can kill and undo reason as well as facilitate transactions and speculations. Global politics depends on the rapid communication between relevant parties, in peace-time and in war. Global culture is electronic culture: as much diaspora as Hollywood. Risk is both represented and managed in the to-ing of fro-ing of public mass-mediated declarations of competing expertise and policy. And if one is to place reflexivity – the capacity to monitor, understand but never quite control the complex dynamics of life in late-modern society, a two-way interaction between thinking and reality as George Soros (1998) describes it – as a central component of what defines those societies as distinctive, then it would seem to me, once again, that it is the media who are the bearers of that reflexivity. Indeed the media are its precondition. They are both the conduits for the representation of public and private thought and action, and its stimulants. For individuals as well as for institutions.

Given my own arguments so far in this book, and making the case, I hope more or less convincingly, for the centrality of media to experience, then it behoves me to consider what implications the media have for an understanding of politics and the exercise of power throughout society, as we move into the next millennium. Indeed given what I have said thus far it would follow that those of us who study the media have a responsibility to engage with the world which has been the object of our attention. The boundary that separates the academy from the world of affairs in this field at least can no longer be defended.

I want in this concluding, but never final, chapter to address some of the questions raised in this multiple confrontation: between the media and the political environment in which they operate and which they frame, as well as that between thought and action. I want to explore the media in politics and the politics of the media. In so doing I will not be offering specific recommendations on policy, and it would be absurd for me to try. It is the ground base, the precondition, for a new media politics that I am after. The challenge is to address what might reasonably be seen as a crisis in global media without resorting to a kind of media fundamentalism. So this is to be the basis of a political project, not a political programme. At its heart is the belief that the study of the media must itself be just such a project.

So, to the questions that such a project has to address, the issues it has to face, the dilemmas it has to resolve. I want to pursue them on the basis of a number of assumptions. These are as follows.

The first is that media technologies, like all other technologies, have the social behind them, the social in front of them and the social embedded in them. We might talk of the media having such and such an effect, and we are not wrong to do so, but it needs to be remembered that media technologies emerge as material and symbolic objects and as catalysts for action, and are effective as such only through the deeds of individuals and institutions. It follows, I believe, that those actions are political. They, of their very nature, involve a struggle over meaning and control: in design, in development, in distribution and in use.

The second is that the media, as cultural forces, are similarly political: subject to conflicts over access and participation; subject to conflicts over rights of ownership and representation; and vulnerable, always, to the uncertainties and the unintended consequences of any and every act of communication. The media connect and separate in one breath. They include and simultaneously exclude. They offer freedoms of expression and claim rights of surveillance and control. They are both enabling and disabling. They create new inequalities, just as they seek to eliminate old ones.

The third is that the media have always been a crucial part of the political process, in democracies as well as tyrannies, for the dissemination and management of information is in turn a crucial part of managing a nation state; and the creation and management of citizenship is in turn dependent on effective information and communication within governments and among the governed as well as between them.

The fourth is that the media are constantly changing, and their relationships to the societies which support them are changing accordingly. This century has arguably been defined by the emergence of electronic media: radio and telephone were there at its beginning, the Internet is there at its end. From valve to transistor, from Morse code to encryption, from the analogue to the digital. And from the local to the global, and back again. From the one to one, to the one to many, and, conceivably now too, in the guise of electronic referenda, e-mails to political leaders and policy-generating on-line fora, from the many to one. From Marconi to Murdoch and Microsoft. From Bell and Baird to Berlusconi and Bertelsmann.

The fifth is that we live in a plural world. We share that world with others. These others are called Simpsons and Ewings, Oprah Winfrey and Dan Leno, Bill Clinton, Tony Blair and Saddam Hussein. They are called Taliban and Tutsi, Bosnians and Serbs. They are the neighbours down the street as well as the nameless on the other side of the globe. We live with them in their difference, both inside and outside the media. No media politics worth its salt can afford to ignore this pluralism. Indeed, it must be the ground on which it is constructed. And no national or global politics can afford to ignore the media.

Such presumptions suggest that we need a fundamental reassessment of the relationship of media to the political process. We live, in Anthony Giddens's (1998) terms, in a global world of states without enemies, and of governance rather than government. It is a world, however, which in its plurality cannot disguise the continuing presence of fundamental difference and conflict, both within states and between them. How is this to be managed? What role can the media play? It is a huge challenge, and one that I will only, at best, be able to begin to outline.

Perhaps I can start by considering some of the ideas and models that have been offered thus far. The first and the most discussed, at least by those who have addressed directly the relationship between the media and the political process, is that of the *public sphere*.

The German philosopher and sociologist Jurgen Habermas (1989) took the notion of the public sphere as the cornerstone for his analysis of the distinctive character of modernity and of its democratic infrastructure, one in which the media played a central role. In his view the public sphere emerged as the bourgeoisie themselves emerged as a distinct and a significant class, as societies industrialized and as markets formed at the end of the eighteenth and the beginning of the nineteenth century. What was at stake was the creation of something called *public opinion* and the possibility for someone called the *citizen* to play a role in the politics of what hitherto had been an exclusive and excluding state.

The public sphere appeared between the realm of the public authority, the state, and that of civil society, comprising the new kinds of private and personal relationships that were being forged in the market-place and in the domestic sphere. The members of this new class, increasingly secure in their wealth and eager to claim the influence in the affairs of the nation that they thought was their due, established the institutions that would enable their presence to be felt in public life. In principal the public sphere was open to all, and all who participated would participate on equal terms. It was the beginning of liberal democracy: round the tables of the coffee-houses, on the pages of the newspapers, which began to provide political commentary as well as news and advertisements, and in the hallowed halls of public museums, libraries and universities. To discuss and to participate. To let reason rule in the affairs of the world. To influence and to command.

The public sphere, as Habermas described it, flowered briefly in Northern Europe, especially in the United Kingdom. Its life was short, quite rapidly compromised and commandeered by the expanding state which became increasingly confident of its ability and rights to intervene in the private lives of its citizens, and by an increasingly powerful and insistent market. The space and time for free and rational debate decreased. The citizen became the consumer, buying ideas, values and beliefs, rather than forging them through discussion. The press lost its bite as it became progressively commercialized. The visual media participated in the creation of what has subsequently been called the society of the spectacle, a kind of refeudalization of public authority which revived the courtly world of image management: of displays of power through person and personality; power performed nightly on the global television screen.

Habermas's ideas have been the source of much debate. There are those who argue that the public sphere was, from the beginning, a fantasy. Habermas saw neither its capacity to exclude (no women, no members of the working class effectively participated), nor the presence of alternative sites and cultures of public debate and action, especially among the working class. He had not read, apparently, his E.P. Thompson (1963). There are others who argue that, despite its historical inaccuracies, many of which Habermas has subsequently acknowledged, his arguments constitute an ideal rather than an idealization, and one which can and must provide the basis for a critique of the failures of contemporary media.

Yet others argue that these same media have, on the contrary, preserved a significant part of what Habermas saw as distinctive in the public sphere: our media, particularly in the guise of public service broadcasting, have offered unparalleled access to public and political life and have done so in ways that enable their discussion in responsive and responsible ways. There are those too who see in the new media, most especially the Internet, opportunities to revive the public sphere in all its imagined glory: for here at last, they say, is a global space for free and informed discussion and debate, and one, crucially, beyond the reach of both commerce and the state.

And there are those, finally, who see in the new media environment no real basis for comparison with what enabled debate and critique at the beginning of the nineteenth century. The bases for effective participation have gone; we no longer live in a world of coffee-houses; our learning is on-line; the world is too complex for us to grasp; we are vulnerable to information overload; and public opinion itself has become a media artefact, to be created and manipulated at will, an ersatz barometer of the well-being of ailing governments or presidents.

What do I want to take from these discussions and debates? Firstly, to recognize the power of the idea and to identify the values that inform it. The argument depends on a belief in the rule of reason and a desire both to protect that rule and to protect those spaces where it can be pursued. At issue is the capacity of media institutions to create and sustain meaningful public debate: accountably, accessibly and responsibly. We cannot ask for, and should not expect, less.

Yet Habermas's version of the public sphere tends to veer overmuch, it might be said, to the singular; and there is a utopian streak in the discussion which of its very nature is prescriptive. This makes the notion of the public sphere curiously, and paradoxically, ahistorical. In his desire to insist on the rule of reason Habermas fails to recognize its plurality and the *different* ways in which public discussions and debates can meaningfully take place. The popular is decried, and in his haste to condemn new forms of privatization and the withdrawal into inner, domestic, not to say suburban, space consequent upon the emergence of the mass media, he misses an opportunity to examine, if only subsequently to condemn, new ways of being and acting in public as well as alternative ways to participate in public discourse.

It is nevertheless this sense of openness that I want to preserve, and reinforce come to that. For the second idea I would like, more briefly, to consider is that of *the open society*. Karl Popper's (1945) great polemic was informed by the massive threat to freedom and to reason which he saw both in the societies of his time and in a significant strand of thinking within Western philosophy. The open society was a society prepared to take risks: to be open to debate and critique, and not closed by the tyrannies of utopian visions, singular ideologies and the concentration of state power. Popper argued against both the morality and practicality of social engineering: the kind of political turn that states, informed by a sense of their own destiny and by their confident belief that they were on the right side of history, adopted as a way of returning the world either to some lost golden age, or to grasp the bright and shining new future. Neo-liberalism and communism in our own time are obvious examples. The problem, for Popper, was historicism: a belief in destiny; and the denial of reason and human difference and fallibility. History, for Popper, has no meaning. Neither history, nor nature, nor one might add technology, can tell us what we ought to do. We live in a world of unintended consequences, where there is no final solution, a world for which we must, in our vulnerability, take responsibility. History is plural. Appeals to a common purpose are fundamentally misconceived and, above all, involve an appeal to abandon reason.

Popper's targets were obvious and in many respects singular: the threat was indeed the threat of the singular, and the power singularity has to mobilize politics and feed the exercise of power. Of course, his own theory depended on a belief in the power of singular reason that would itself, now, be open to challenge. Yet he lived in and through a totalitarian world. We, for the most part, do not. And in thinking through some of the implications of his work for an understanding of the exercise of power in high modern society, and of course, for media's role within that, we have to engage, perforce, with a more complex environment. It is arguably the case that present dangers are not those only of the singular, but of the unlimited plural. Anything goes. We may fear the constraints on action and belief posed by domineering and dominating ideology, be its source in the activities of the state or in the fundamentalism of a belief in the global market, but we are also confronted by the fragmentation of moral and political life, reduced to the supposedly incommensurable beliefs and values of individuals and groups. Identity politics. The politics of individualism. These pose, it might be argued, as much a threat to freedom as any totalitarian ideology. Too quick an acceptance of the rights of others is often a mask for unthinking and unreason. We can understand but we cannot judge. And anything goes.

The mass media created a mass society. Mass society was a vulnerable society. Atomized individuals at risk. Propaganda was the great fear. Radio was its instrument. Authoritarian societies exercised power through the media, via direct control of both institutions and agendas. Now the fear is the opposite. Our media provide everything and nothing. The market rules, and within the market *we* are the kings and queens. Both fears are exaggerated of course. Both are true.

A contemporary politics of the media, a politics of new media, has to steer a path between the Scylla of the totalitarian and the Charybdis of the unlimited plural. It is not necessarily *the* third way. I need to return to both Isaiah Berlin and Emmanuel Levinas.

At the risk of distorting two distinct and original philosophical contributions, I want to suggest that both these thinkers offer a similar position, grounded, it must be said, in a deep and, in the best sense of the word, a liberal, humanism, in turn based on a fundamental respect for the Other. Both recognize the irreducibility of Otherness. Both insist on a plural universe. Both, equally, require the effort to reach the Other through an acceptance of a common humanity. For Berlin, this is what distinguishes pluralism from relativism. Defending both Herder and Vico from the latter charge, Berlin has this to say. I quote him, for the last time, at length:

> They are inviting us to look at societies different from our own, the ultimate values of which we can perceive to be wholly understandable ends of life for men who are different, indeed from us, but human beings, *semblables*, into whose circumstances we can, by a great effort which we are commanded to make, find a way, 'enter', to use Vico's term. . . . If the quest is successful, we shall see that the values of these remote peoples are such as human beings like ourselves – creatures capable of conscious intellectual and moral discrimination – could live by. These values may attract or repel us: but to understand a past culture is to understand how men like ourselves, in a particular natural or man-made environment, could embody them in their activities, and why; by dint of enough historical investigation and imaginative sympathy, to see how human (that is intelligible) lives could be lived by pursuing them. (Berlin, 1990: 79, 82–3)

Pluralism presumes the possibility of such understanding despite difference. It is not relativism because it presumes a common humanity through which both identification and judgements can be made. This does not involve the imposition of a single moral code, but an acceptance that human beings are defined by, and can be judged against, that which makes them human. And for Berlin, for Levinas and for Baumann the Other can, most certainly, be wrong.

Understanding cannot be morally neutral because understanding is based on identification of common humanity and the rights of others. We will not understand if we ignore those differences, either by erasing them or by subsuming them. The Other, as Levinas argues, is like us but not like us. The Other must be recognized, confronted, appreciated, understood. To repeat, our humanity is the consequence of our recognition of that primary responsibility, not its cause.

The stranger, 'the wanderer who comes today and stays tomorrow', the one who is remote yet close by, who is close by yet remote, in Georg Simmel's characterization of him, is a key figure for late-modern society even more than he was at the beginning of this century. This stranger is close to us 'insofar as we feel between him and ourselves similarities of nationality or social position, of occupation or of general human nature. He is far from us insofar as these similarities extend beyond him and us, and connect us only because they connect a great many people' (Simmel, 1971: 147).

This dialectic of distance and closeness, of familiarity and strangeness, is the crucial articulation of the late-modern world, and it is a dialectic in which the media are crucially implicated. Indeed it might be suggested, albeit in an entirely abstract and easily trivialized way, that this is the media's project *par excellence*. As I have argued, the media are central to our experience of the world, and it is in their reach, through space and time, that that experience is either enriched or impoverished by images and ideas, words and worlds, to which we would otherwise have no access. This perception is also what grounds the media as global, and which insists on the media's centrality to an understanding of global culture, society and polity.

What are the implications of these observations, then, for a new media politics? On what issues must we now pronounce?

They are, of course, legion. No part of contemporary social life is untouched by media presence. And its absence is felt like a wound. In a so-called information society the absence of information is seen to be deprivation beyond measure. Yet even this so often articulated perception is a mistake. Information is valueless. Knowledge is what counts. We need to be cautious in the face of arguments which see in the growing division between the information rich and the information poor an inevitable and necessary social evil. When huge swathes of people are without telephones and televisions it is hard to bewail the absence of the Internet. Yet in all these cases the technologies are not, by themselves, creative. Access to both local and global communication networks is, certainly, enabling, but we have to have something to say, and there has to be someone to listen, and to hear. Can we not talk of the communication rich and the communication poor, the knowledge rich and the knowledge poor instead? Can we not think beyond our own sense of what counts as a valuable, if not an essential, commodity? Technology can only complement and enhance social and cultural life when there is already something of value to complement and to enhance.

For we know how alienating the world has become. We are alienated, increasingly and perhaps above all, from the political process, deprived of meaningful participation in it by the very technologies which continually inform us of its inner workings. How, in the end, can we vote for an image? Will the new world of intelligent agents and avatars mean anything at all? How can I respond electronically to a request for my opinion on a political matter if I do not understand what I am being asked to adjudicate? To ask such questions is not Luddism. On the contrary. Many are now thinking about ways of involving new media technologies in the revival of national, and the stimulation of global, politics. There are those who see in the interactivity of a global network the opportunity to revive existing democratic structures, and to enable individuals (albeit only those who have access to a terminal and know how to use it, and why) to respond to, or even maybe initiate, dialogue with political leaders and governments. There are others who see in these same technologies an opportunity to create new forms of political participation entirely, new structures and new kinds of (self) governance. There are those, on the other hand, who see in the enormous range and reach of the new media significant opportunities for closing down freedoms and for unparalleled surveillance, both economic and political. These options, these threats, these questions, are of course too important to be left either to the technologists or the politicians.

Likewise the politics of risk. And here too the media are both tools and troubles. My sense is that all societies and all individuals throughout history have had to deal with risk, and that in the experience of everyday life there is little to distinguish the supposed risks generated by the excesses of biomedical engineering or global warming from the failures of crops and the threats of the devil. Whereas earlier societies had their shamans, we have our news readers. There has been little concerted work designed to make sense of the media's role in the management of risk, yet its centrality can hardly be denied. One study that did (Turner et al., 1986), examined life on the San Andreas fault, revealing a finely balanced cycle of risk-reporting and anxiety management in news and current affairs. Reports of the latest 'scientific' findings and predictions alternated with debunking or other reassuring strategies in such a way that the issue was never lost sight of, but was never allowed to get out of hand (that is, until it actually did in 1988). The new media politics, just like the old, must understand its own significance for the conduct and security of everyday life. If we are to avoid a politics of panic, such as was experienced in the UK during the BSE episode, then we have to address, directly and insistently, the machinery not just of government, but of the context in which government takes place, and which in turn constrains it. That is, in matters of public policy and effective governance, the media are both context and text: here at last we might wish to take a version of Marshall McLuhan's dictum that the medium is *also* the message to heart.

And likewise the politics of inclusion. How can the media be used to enable participation in political life without exclusion? In a world in which minorities, both objectively and subjectively defined, are being encouraged to seize their time and their identity, and in which the media are equally often seen as crucial instruments for both, how to avoid a parochial and defensive politics of self-definition and self-interest? How to avoid those with shared or shareable views, or values speaking only to themselves as a kind of self-creating and self-sustaining, electronically mediated cultural ghetto? How to avoid that denial of the Other, and of the shock of, and the responsibility for, the Other in which such ghettoization inevitably will result? How to bridge the society of the excluded middle, in which more or less inclusive institutions, until recently the preserve of the state and with broadcasting crucially among them, are disappearing under the combined threats of global markets, fragmenting media space and local and minority interests? How to make the stranger feel at home?

Much is made in current discussions of new media politics of the continuing need for regulation: of markets, competition, content, especially in the light of the increasing domination of the global industry by a handful of multinational corporations. The case is a cogent one, at least as far as the market and competition are concerned, though it is difficult to implement since national governments cannot control their media space as they once believed they could, and there is no responsive international structure within which to agree policies oriented either to regulation or to rights. Indeed it could be argued that in a world of media publishing, as opposed to broadcasting, such regulation can only be pursued on the basis of existing anti-trust legislation of a kind relevant to any move towards monopolization in whatever industry.

But there is more to new media politics than debates about regulation. I want to suggest that education is just as important, and by education, in this context, I mean media literacy. We need to know, all of us, how the media work and we need to know how to read and understand what we see and hear. This is our project, of course; for those of us who study the media must also pass on what we learn. But given the electronic media's ubiquity and centrality to everyday life, given its salience to our everyday project of making sense of the world we live in, nothing less will do.

Politics has to be both thought and practice. Media politics is no exception. Politics and the media both depend on trust. We study the media because we need to understand how they contribute to the exercise of power in late-modern society, both within the established political process and without it. The media have a responsibility to make the world intelligible, no more, no less. For it is only in its intelligibility that the world and the others who live in it become human. And those of us who study the media must make the media intelligible. It is a project that is neither easy nor comfortable. But we pursue it in the hope that by placing a grain of sand in an oyster the irritation caused by our presumption will, from time to time, turn to pearl.

References

Adorno, Theodor (1954) 'Television and the patterns of mass culture', in Bernard Rosenberg and David Manning White (eds), *Mass Culture: the Popular Arts in America*, New York, Free Press, pp. 474–88.
Anderson, Benedict (1983) *Imagined Communities: Reflections on the Origin and Spread of Nationalism*, London, Verso.
Ang, Ien (1986) *Watching Dallas Soap: Opera and the Melodramatic Imagination*, London, Routledge.
Appadurai, Arjun (1996) *Modernity at Large: Cultural Dimensions of Globalization*, Minneapolis, Minnesota University Press.
Aristotle (1963) *Poetics*, Everyman's Library, London, J.M. Dent.
Bachelard, Gaston (1964) *The Poetics of Space*, Boston, MA, Beacon Press.
Barthes, Roland (1972) *Mythologies*, London, Jonathan Cape.
Barthes, Roland (1976) *The Pleasure of the Text*, London, Jonathan Cape.
Barthes, Roland (1977) *Image–Music–Text: Essays Selected and Translated by Stephen Heath*, London, Fontana.
Barthes, Roland (1981) *Camera Lucida: Reflections on Photography*, London, Jonathan Cape.
Baudrillard, Jean (1988) *Selected Writings*, edited and introduced by Mark Poster, Cambridge, Polity Press.
Baudrillard, Jean (1995) *The Gulf War did not Take Place*, Sydney, Power Publications.
Baumann, Zygmunt (1989) *Modernity and the Holocaust*, Cambridge, Polity Press.
Baumann, Zygmunt (1993) *Postmodern Ethics*, Cambridge, Polity Press.
Beck, Ulrich (1992) *Risk Society*, London, Sage.
Benjamin, Walter (1970) *Illuminations*, London, Fontana.
Benjamin, Walter (1976) *Charles Baudelaire: A Lyric Poet in the Era of High Capitalism*, London, Verso.
Berlin, Isaiah (1990) *The Crooked Timber of Humanity*, London, John Murray.
Berlin, Isaiah (1997) *The Proper Study of Mankind*, London, Chatto and Windus.
Billig, Michael (1987) *Arguing and Thinking: a Rhetorical Approach to Social Psychology*, Cambridge, Cambridge University Press.
Burke, Kenneth (1955) *A Rhetoric of Motives*, New York, George Brazillier.
Burke, Peter (1978) *Popular Culture in Early Modern Europe*, London, Maurice Temple Smith.
Butler, Judith (1990) *Gender Trouble: Feminism and the Subversion of Identity*, London, Routledge.
Caillois, Roger (1962) *Man, Play and Games*, Glencoe, IL, Free Press.

Cairncross, Frances (1997) *The Death of Distance: How the Communications Revolution Will Change our Lives*, London, Orion Business Books.

Carey, James (1989) *Communication as Culture: Essays on Media and Society*, Boston, MA, Unwin Hyman.

Castells, Manuel (1996) *The Rise of the Network Society*, Oxford, Basil Blackwell.

Chaney, David (1983) 'A symbolic mirror of ourselves: civic ritual in mass society', *Media, Culture & Society*, 5 (2): 119–36.

Cicero (1942) *De Oratore*, 2 vols, Loeb Classical Library, Cambridge, MA, Harvard University Press.

Cohen, Anthony (1985) *The Symbolic Construction of Community*, Chichester and London, Ellis Harwood and Tavistock.

Cohen, Stanley (1972) *Folk Devils and Moral Panics*, London, McGibbon and Kee.

Culler, Jonathan (1975) *Structuralist Poetics: Structuralism, Linguistics and the Study of Literature*, London, Routledge and Kegan Paul.

Dasgupta, Partha (1988) 'Trust as a commodity', in Diego Gambetta (ed.), *Trust: Making and Breaking Cooperative Relations*, Oxford, Basil Blackwell, pp. 49–72.

Davis, Colin (1996) *Levinas: an Introduction*, Cambridge, Polity Press.

Dayan, Daniel (1998) 'Particularist media and diasporic communications', in Tamar Liebes and James Curran (eds), *Media, Ritual and Identity*, London, Routledge, pp. 103–13.

Debord, Guy (1977) *The Society of the Spectacle*, London, Practical Paradise Productions.

Diamond, Elin (ed.) (1996) *Performance and Cultural Politics*, London, Routledge.

Diamond, Elin (1997) *Unmaking Mimesis*, London, Routledge.

Elias, Norbert (1978) *The Civilising Process, Vol. 1: The History of Manners*, Oxford, Blackwell.

Frith, Simon (1983) 'The pleasures of the hearth', in *Formations of Pleasure*, London, Routledge and Kegan Paul, pp. 101–23.

Gambetta, Diego (ed.) (1988) *Trust: Making and Breaking Cooperative Relations*, Oxford, Basil Blackwell.

Garfinkel, Harold (1967) *Studies in Ethnomethodology*, Englewood Cliffs, NJ, Prentice-Hall.

Gell, Alfred (1988) 'Technology and magic', *Anthropology Today*, 4 (2): 6–9.

Gerbner, George (1986) 'Living with television: the dynamics of the culturation process', in J. Bryant and D. Zillman (eds), *Perspectives on Media Effects*, Hillside, NJ, Lawrence Erlbaum, pp. 17–40.

Giddens, Anthony (1990) *The Consequences of Modernity*, Cambridge, Polity Press.

Giddens, Anthony (1991) *Modernity and Self-identity: Self and Society in the Late Modern Age*, Cambridge, Polity Press.

Giddens, Anthony (1998) *The Third Way: the Renewal of Social Democracy*, Cambridge, Polity Press.

Gillespie, Marie (1995) *Television, Ethnicity and Cultural Change*, London, Routledge.

Gray, John (1998) *False Dawn: the Delusions of Global Capitalism*, London, Granta Books.

Habermas, Jurgen (1970) 'Towards a theory of communicative competence', in Hans Peter Dreitzel (ed.), *Recent Sociology No. 2*, New York, Macmillan, pp. 114–50.

Habermas, Jurgen (1989) *The Structural Transformation of the Public Sphere: an Inquiry into a Category of Bourgeois Society*, Cambridge, Polity Press.

Hall, Stuart, Critcher, Charles, Jefferson, Tony, Clarke, John and Robert, Brian (1978) *Policing the Crisis: Mugging, the State and Law and Order*, London, Macmillan.

Haraway, Donna J. (1985/1991) *Simians, Cyborgs, and Women*, London, Free Association Books.

Hartmann, Geoffrey (1997) 'The cinema animal', in Yosefa Loshitsky (ed.), *Spielberg's Holocaust: Critical Perspectives on Schindler's List*, Bloomington, Indiana University Press, pp. 61–76.

Hastrup, Kirsten (1995) *A Passage to Anthropology: Between Experience and Theory*, London, Routledge.

Heller, Agnes (1984) *Everyday Life*, London, Routledge and Kegan Paul.

Horkheimer, Max and Adorno, Theodor (1972) *Dialectic of Enlightenment*, New York, Seabury Press.

Huizinga, Jan (1970/1949) *Homo Ludens*, London, Maurice Temple Smith.

Innes, Harold (1972) *Empire and Communications*, Toronto, University of Toronto Press.

Jhally, Sut (1990) *The Codes of Advertising: Fetishism and the Political Economy of Meaning in Consumer Society*, London, Routledge.

Katz, Elihu and Lazarsfeld, Paul (1955) *Personal Influence: the Part Played by People in Mass Communication*, New York, Free Press.

Kraut, Robert (1998) 'Internet paradox: a social technology that reduces social investment and psychological well being', *American Psychologist*, 53 (9): 1017–31.

Levinas, Emmanuel (1987) *Time and the Other*, Pittsburgh, PA, Duquesne University Press.

Lewis, C.A. (1942) *Broadcasting from Within*, London, Newnes.

Liebes, Tamar and Katz, Elihu (1990) *The Export of Meaning*, Oxford, Oxford University Press.

Livingstone, Sonia (1998) 'Mediated childhoods: a comparative approach to young peoples' changing media environments in Europe', *European Journal of Communication*, 13 (4): 435–56.

McGinniss, Joe (1970) *The Selling of a President*, London, Deutsch.

McKeon, Richard (1987) *Rhetoric: Essays in Invention and Discovery*, Woodbridge, CT, Ox Bow Press.

McLuhan, Marshall (1964) *Understanding Media*, London, Routledge and Kegan Paul.

Mansell, Robin (1996) 'Designing electronic commerce', in Robin Mansell and Roger Silverstone (eds), *Communication by Design: the Politics of Information and Communication Technologies*, Oxford, Oxford University Press, pp. 103–28.

Marx, Karl and Engels, Frederick (1970) *The German Ideology*, London, Lawrence and Wishart.

Mass Observation (1939) *Britain*, Harmondsworth, Penguin.

Mercer, Kobena (1996) *Imagined Communities*, Manchester, National Touring Exhibitions/Cornerhouse Productions.

Meyrowitz, Joshua (1985) *No Sense of Place: the Impact of Electronic Media on Social Behaviour*, New York, Oxford University Press.

Negroponte, Nicholas (1995) *Being Digital: the Road Map for Survival on the Information Superhighway*, London, Hodder and Stoughton.

Ong, Walter (1982) *Orality and Literacy: the Technologizing of the Word*, London, Methuen.

Popper, Karl (1945) *The Open Society and its Enemies*, 2 vols, London, Routledge and Kegan Paul.

Renov, Michael (1993) *Theorizing Documentary*, London, Routledge.

Rheingold, Harold (1994) *The Virtual Community: Finding Connection in a Computerised World*, London, Secker and Warburg.

Ricoeur, Paul (1984) *Time and Narrative, Vol. 1*, Chicago, IL, Chicago University Press.

Samuel, Raphael (1994) *Theatres of Memory, Vol. 1: Past and Present in Contemporary Culture*, London, Verso.

Scannell, Paddy (1988) 'Radio times: the temporal arrangements of broadcasting in the modern world', in Phillip Drummond and Richard Pateson (eds), *Television and its Audience: International Research Perspectives*, London, British Film Institute.

Silverstone, Roger (1981) *The Message of Television: Myth and Narrative in Contemporary Culture*, London: Heinemann Educational Books.

Silverstone, Roger (1994) *Television and Everyday Life*, London, Routledge.

Silverstone, Roger (1998) 'Jewish television: prospects and possibilities', JPR Policy Paper, no. 1, March, London, Institute for Jewish Policy Research.

Simmel, Georg (1971/1908) 'The stranger', in Donald E. Levine (ed.), *Georg Simmel: On Individuality and Social Forms*, Chicago, IL, Chicago University Press, pp. 143–9.

Soros, George (1998) *The Crisis of Global Capitalism: Open Society Endangered*, London, Little, Brown and Co.

Steiner, George (1975) *After Babel*, Oxford, Oxford University Press.

Thompson, E.P. (1963) *The Making of the English Working Class*, London, Gollancz.

Thompson, E.P. (1971) 'The moral economy of the English crowd in the eighteenth century', *Past and Present* 50: 76–136.

Todorov, Tzvetan (1977) *Theories of the Symbol*, Oxford, Blackwell.

Todorov, Tzvetan (1981) *Introduction to Politics*, Minneapolis, Minnesota University Press.

Turner, Ralph, Nigg, Joanne M. and Paz, Denise (1986) *Waiting for Disaster: Earthquake Watch in California*, Berkeley, California University Press.

Turner, Victor (1969) *The Ritual Process*, London, Routledge and Kegan Paul.

Van Gennep, Arnold (1960) *The Rites of Passage*, London, Routledge and Kegan Paul.

Williams, Raymond (1974) *Television: Technology and Cultural Form*, London, Fontana.

Winnicott, D.W. (1974) *Playing and Reality*, Harmondsworth, Penguin.

Wolfe, Thomas (1971) *Of Time and the River*, Harmondsworth, Penguin.

Yates, Frances A. (1964) *Giordano Bruno and the Hermetic Tradition*, London, Routledge and Kegan Paul.

Yates, Frances (1966) *The Art of Memory*, London, Routledge and Kegan Paul.

Young, James E. (1990) *Writing and Rewriting the Holocaust: Narrative and the Consequences of Interpretation*, Bloomington, Indiana University Press.
Young, James E. (1993) *The Texture of Memory: Holocaust Memorials and Meaning*, New Haven, CT, Yale University Press.
Zelizer, Barbie (1997) 'Every once in a while: *Schindler's List* and the shaping of history', in Yosefa Loshitsky (ed.), *Spielberg's Holocaust: Critical Perspectives on Schindler's List*, Bloomington, Indiana University Press, pp. 18–40.
Zucker, Lynne (1986) 'Production of trust: institutional sources of economic structure, 1840–1920', in B.M. Shaw and L.L. Cummings (eds), *Research in Organisational Behavior*, Vol. 8, Greenwich, CT, JAI Press, pp. 53–111.

Index

Printed in the United States
33750LVS00004B/1-84

9 780761 964544